Formation for Evangelization

Formation for Evangelization

Reflections of a Catholic Educator

James T. Mulligan, CSC

NOVALIS

Formation for Evangelization: Reflections of a Catholic Educator is published by Novalis.

Cover and layout: Gilles Lepine

© 1994, Novalis, St. Paul University, Ottawa, Canada

Business Office: Novalis,
   49 Front St. East, 2nd Floor,Toronto, Ontario, M5E 1B3

Editorial Office: Novalis,
   223 Main Street, Ottawa, Ontario, K1S 1C4

Legal deposit: 3rd trimester, 1994
   National Library of Canada
   Bibliothèque nationale du Québec

Printed in Canada.

Canadian Cataloguing in Publication Data

Mulligan, James T. (James Terrence), 1942-

   Formation for evangelization: Reflections of a Catholic educator

Includes bibliographical references and index.

ISBN: 2-89088-676-X

   1. Catholic high school teachers—Training of—Canada.
   2. Evangelistic work—Canada. 3. Catholic Church—Education—Canada. I. Title.

LC504.M85 1994   377'.8271   C94-900589-4

NOVALIS

Contents

Part One: The Problem

A reflection of a priest-educator
on the most critical issue facing Catholic education

Part Two:
The Foundations for a Model of Formation

A reflection from a reading of the signs of the times

Part Three: The Model

Reflections from a formation journal

To the scores and scores
of committed Catholic educators across Canada
for whom teaching in the Catholic school
is more vocation than job:
that the spirit of resistance
and
the hope in God's present activity in our life situation
might continue to sustain them
in all the wintry seasons
they may pass through.

In Appreciation

I acknowledge, first and foremost, the teachers who journeyed with me in this formation experience: Ann, Arthur, Donna, Gregory, Joseph, Marie, Mario, Marisa, Michael and Raymond. Their generosity of spirit, interest in Catholic education, and dedication to this project were both humbling and profoundly gratifying for me. As a long-time practitioner of the ministry of Catholic education, I have had my hopes rekindled and my ideals recharged by being an eavesdropper-researcher in their presence.

I have fashioned this book from my Doctor of Ministry thesis: *A Model of Formation for Teachers in the Catholic High School,* submitted to the Toronto School of Theology. I am deeply indebted to Carl Starkloff, SJ, of Regis College, the director of my thesis. I would also like to acknowledge the encouragement of Mary Malone of St. Jerome's College, University of Waterloo, a reader of the thesis, who urged that I make this research available to the wider Catholic education community.

I am especially indebted to Bill, Bob, Eileen and Eileen, Frank, John and Thérèse—Catholic educators all—whose company I shared for three years in an ongoing reflection on the doing—the ministry—of Catholic education in our time and place. Our experience together as a group of pilgrim believers concerned about Catholic education confirms again for me the fundamental intuition that ministry in the church today is most effective and most satisfying when it is done in the context of a caring, critiquing, enabling community.

Finally, to two friends I extend very special thanks. Eileen McCarthy, my colleague at Notre Dame College School, Welland, offered her usual insightful critique and editorial genius to the preparation of this text. Reverend Joseph Mahoney, a pastor emeritus in the Diocese of St. Catharines, was most helpful in the questions and suggestions he proposed for improving the text.

Introduction

This book is about the formation of Catholic teachers. I believe that the formation of Catholic teachers—both initial formation and ongoing formation—is the most pressing question in Catholic education in our time.

As I did in my earlier study on the Catholic high school, I ground this reflection on the urgency of formation in my own day-to-day practice as a Catholic educator. While my experience happens to be in the Catholic *high* school, I am confident that the vision, spirit, questions and strategies that I offer in these pages are applicable for all Catholic educators and adaptable to all Catholic schools—whether they be elementary or secondary. My own experience, too, is rooted in the Catholic separate schools of the province of Ontario. Thus I write from that experience. But again, based on conversations and encounters with Catholic educators in Alberta, Saskatchewan and Newfoundland, my hunch is that their Catholic education experience is similar; that the questions, analyses and responses raised in this study are common to Catholic separate schools and Catholic teachers across Canada.

Undoubtedly the mid-1990s are challenging times for Catholic education. In the Province of Ontario we are now some five years into *the moment* of the Ontario Bishops' *This Moment of Promise* (their 1989 pastoral letter on Catholic education). It appears that as the months and years of this moment slip by, the entire Catholic education project becomes more complex and uncertain. The current moment in Catholic education, fraught with so many new questions and fresh ambiguities, contains within it more than a few daunting challenges for every Catholic educator.

Governments everywhere, taking up the neo-conservative mantra of debt reduction, globalization and increased competitiveness, are down-sizing and rationalizing. In Ontario, a social contract has been deemed an inescapable way to confront what the provincial government considers an intolerable deficit. In the public sector of education, the social contract means cuts in spending and a decreased number of teachers in our classrooms. For Catholic schools, this could mean in addition fewer chaplains in the high schools and fewer faith-life animators and religious education consultants at Catholic education centres. It could also mean a larger pupil-teacher ratio (PTR) in our religion classes and decreased funding for retreats. In a word, the religious or faith dimension of our schools cannot escape taking a budgetary hit. This hurts our efforts at evangelization.

In Ontario, a restructuring of education is also under way. *Outcome-based education, holistic curriculum, de-streaming, activity-based learning* are some of the phrases used to describe the current provincial approach to education. But this "new" approach means that classroom teachers must dedicate more time and energy to creating new strategies and new units of curriculum. It means, as well, that most professional development in the last two years has been devoted to the preparation of teachers for the new educational reality.

Restricted budgets mean less money. If budgets reflect priorities, then separate school boards face enormous challenges to find *concrete* ways—beyond mission statements, policy statements and other rhetoric—to be trustees of their unique and sacred trust: the Catholicity of our schools. Similarly, board administrations and principals, responsible for the implementation of Ministry of Education policies, are also enormously challenged: for example, that *Transition Years* does not mean no time for Catholicity, evangelization, faith formation. (*Transition Years* is the most recent Ontario Ministry of Education policy governing the structuring of programming during the intermediate years.) It's not "either-or." It must be "both-and." The indictment we risk is that constraints of money or time may cause the focus on Catholicity and all that entails to be placed on the back burner. And *the moment of promise* may continue to slip and slide away!

The old question of the *existence* of Catholic education in Ontario even comes back into play during our current moment. Most of us thought that Bill 30 and full funding settled the constitutional legitimacy of publicly funded Catholic schools in Ontario. But the recently constituted *Royal Commission on Learning* (May 1993) has as its mandate to review in a comprehensive way all aspects of education in Ontario. This review will include questions such as: Are there too many school boards? Where is there overlapping? Should school boards merge? Questions like these can be unsettling for Catholic educators because they could touch on our autonomy and present mode of existence.

Finally, teachers in the classroom absorb the full impact of the pressures and stresses deriving from the present moment's very difficult economic and social context. Teachers are educators, but increasingly they are called to be social workers and proxy parents. And for many of our Catholic students, Catholic teachers are expected to be the primary role model and educator in the faith — duties in the past reserved to parents and parish.

All of this cannot but contribute to the complexity and ambiguity of doing Catholic education in the current moment.

The present moment is tremendously challenging and urgently needs teachers who are committed in faith to the Lord Jesus; teachers who are committed to being followers of Jesus in the Roman Catholic Christian community. I believe that the different challenges inherent in our contemporary social and ecclesial context mean that the faith education and formation of our teachers must become the first priority for all of the partners in Catholic education—teachers, trustees, administrators, parents and pastoral leaders. The urgency of formation becomes even more obvious when one considers that, within a decade, hundreds of experienced, dedicated teachers will retire from our Catholic schools. It is not so much a question of who will take their place: there are more than enough young teachers now seeking teaching positions. Rather, the critical questions are: What sort of formation will these teachers have to teach in *Catholic* schools? How ready will they be to evangelize in our schools? What will be their understanding of the *vocation* of the Catholic teacher? What means will they have to develop and deepen their understanding of that vocation?

My intention in writing this book is threefold. First of all, I want to draw attention to the urgency of the formation question. The Bishops' *moment* is passing. Eventually we are going to deplete all of the months and years that make up *this moment.* But what about the *promise?* How *Catholic* are our schools and our boards? How *committed* are our teachers? How *effective* is the evangelization in our schools? All of these questions, I believe, can be reduced to one question: how *prepared* are our teachers to teach and to continue to teach in a *Catholic* school? I have been preoccupied with this formation question since my study on the Catholic high school, *Evangelization and the Catholic High School* (Novalis, 1990). The questions of *readiness* and *vocation awareness* constituted a sub-text throughout that book: how to evangelize the evangelizers. My recent experience with Catholic educators across Canada—teachers, trustees, administrators, parents, clergy—has only heightened the sense of urgency I feel about the formation question. It is the Catholic teacher in particular who must be the beneficiary of our formation strategies.

Secondly, I want to propose what I believe is a *credible, doable, affordable* model for forming teachers in our Catholic schools. The model described in this book is both a realistic way to introduce beginning teachers into a reflection on the vocation of Catholic educator and an effective means to have experienced teachers continue to reflect on their own practice as Catholic educator.

Thirdly, I want to offer, through the different snap-shots of the present Catholic education reality developed in this reflection, an up-to-date, critical look at where we find ourselves today in the doing of Catholic education. I believe that this data can make a useful contribution to colleagues elsewhere in Canada who, in their passion for Catholic education, are preoccupied with the formation question or with similar questions.

In my experience, teachers in our Catholic schools fall into one of four groups. There seems to be one group of teachers for whom the vocation dimension of teaching in a Catholic school means very little. Teaching is a job. They are professionals. There is, for them, very little if any difference between teaching in a Catholic school and teaching in a public school.

In contrast to these teachers are the teachers for whom the ministry of Catholic education and the vocation to teach in the Catholic school are central to their identity as teacher. This group of teachers is the present salvation and the future hope for maintaining and developing *the Catholic character* of our schools. These teachers, I am convinced, are the reason why there continues to be *promise* in our present moment. Such teachers graciously appreciate the many gifts and joys that are part and parcel of teaching in a Catholic school. And they accept, too, with determined resistance, the questions, failures, contradictions and challenges that are all wrapped up in the *struggle* dimension of Catholic education.

And then there is the group in-between. It seems to me that many teachers in this group could be open to embracing more sincerely the *vocation* dimension of Catholic educator; many of them could be receptive to different experiences of continuing faith formation. But they are now waiting out the present moment—waiting to be challenged; waiting to be encouraged; waiting to be invited.

The fourth group is the entry-level group of teachers. As in any profession, beginning teachers are generally influenced by their more experienced peers in the profession. I believe that new teachers in our Catholic schools are looking for models and will inevitably find a model in one or other of the groups I have described.

Formation must be the priority for each of the four groups of teachers. For the first group, if there is no discernible difference between a Catholic school and a public school, then the whole Catholic education project is simply a sham, a duplication of scarce tax dollars, and should be discontinued. Teachers in this group must be challenged to see that the theological ideals of our vision statements *can be* lived out and real-ized in a school community and that it is in the struggle to live out and real-ize these ideals that the difference between a Catholic school and a public school can be found.

As for the committed teachers, the evangelizers must continue to be evangelized. These teachers deserve further formation: the opportunity to reflect in faith on the *why* and the *how* of their vocation as Catholic teacher. Not to have ongoing faith formation is to risk discouragement and burn-out. Indeed, it is to use up very quickly and recklessly Catholic education's most precious resource—the rich human commitment that is really the heart of this moment of promise.

The in-between group, I find, can make the qualitative difference in any school. Schools that have an exceptional spirit and stand out because of the positive human relations between students and staff, the quantity and quality of co-curricular activities, the genuineness of its academic life for students of all levels, and a community faith-life driven by the articulated desire to know and love Jesus and to serve Jesus who is especially present in the poor and disadvantaged—these are schools in which a considerable number of the in-between group of teachers have thrown their lot in with the committed group of teachers. And this happens, I believe, because formation and ongoing faith education for staff have had a high priority for the leaders of such schools.

For entry-level teachers, religion courses at faculties of education and the Part One Ontario English Catholic Teachers' Association (OECTA) religion course required by most boards are essential and are usually very helpful in introducing novice teachers to the Catholic education experience. But I am convinced that such courses, while absolutely necessary, are still inadequate by themselves in meeting the various challenges contained in the current moment of Catholic education. Further formation of a practical ongoing nature is necessary to assist beginning teachers, as they personalize their own vocations as Catholic teachers.

In this book I take the stance of reflective practitioner. For me, this identification means nothing more than to be a follower of Jesus, who has the habit of looking critically at the grace moments and sin moments in my work as a Catholic educator. In Part One, I reflect in autobiographical fashion on my own pilgrimage as a priest-educator. I belong to a religious community that has made and continues to make an important contribution to Catholic education in Canada and the United States. As a student, I was formed in the Christian education charism of the Congregation of Holy Cross. As a teacher, I have worked out of the vision and energy of this charism for more than two decades. I have also experienced the dramatic changes that have reshaped Catholic education in the last ten years. In my reflections on my own journey I conclude that there is a formation void. This is our present and future problem. The buildings, the money, the state-of-the-art technology and progressive educational philosophies and programs that make up the superstructure of publicly funded Catholic schools all risk crumbling or at best merely duplicating public education because our own foundation for Catholic schools is so fragile. That foundation is the initial and continuing formation of teachers to teach in a Catholic school.

In Part Two, I share a reflection on the present and future of Catholic education based on my own questioning and reading concerning the formation question. I call the ideas I develop in this section "Foundations." Understandings of the church, of the relationship of the church to Catholic education, of evangelization, of what constitutes an English Canadian Catholic culture, of formation—these are the ideas that become the basis or framework for the model of formation that I propose in this book. For me these are significant ideas. They are critical to my own intellectual pilgrimage as a practitioner in that they provide me with a sharper focus, increased clarity and a deeper grasp of the many dimensions of the formation problem.

A special note about Part Two. No doubt many in Catholic education who share my preoccupation with the pressing need for teacher formation may initially lack the time or the inclination to explore the foundations. Please, freely go directly to Part Three, on the model of formation which is the core and reason for this book. I include the foundations because I want to acknowledge *how* certain ideas have unwittingly led me from search to inspiration, and because I want to introduce certain of these ideas and their authors, even if by far-too-brief selections or summaries, to individuals who may already be embarked on similar searches of their own. I am confident, too, that a familiarity with these foundations could be very beneficial for student teachers who are in faculties of education. And I hope that having read about and perhaps then tried this proposed experience in formation, that there will be new "others" in the Catholic education community, who will join the search for ways to enable us all to deepen our competence and commitment as teachers in Catholic schools. Part Two can then become a meeting place for some companions on their search.

I get to the heart of my reflection on the formation question in Part Three with a description of a very practical, relevant formation experience. In these chapters I report on a journey I made with ten Catholic educators as they engaged in a year-long conversation about the *meaning* and the *doing* of Catholic education in our present moment. Five of these teachers are beginning teachers; five are more experienced teachers, firmly committed to *the promise*—to the possibilities and ideals embodied in Catholic education. In this report, I look at the teachers as they look at themselves in this uncertain, confusing, yet challenging and exciting moment in Catholic education. I present some very honest and spirited analysis and critique, as well as some very real, pertinent and encouraging examples of evangelization in a Catholic school. In the course of this conversation, *interpretation* takes on special meaning for the formation of Catholic teachers. The Catholic teacher must become an *interpreter*—one who can make sense out of the many conflicting ideas and practices inherent in our present social and ecclesial context. Thus, teachers must make their own both the spirit of, and the skills for, interpretation. They must do this for their own well-being and peace of mind as Catholic educators. At the same time, teachers are invited to become a resource for their students, to introduce their students confidently to ways the contemporary Christian can go about "acting justly, loving kindly, and walking humbly with your God" (Micah 6:8). This conversation between beginning and experienced teachers proves to be a very relevant, practical and affordable experience in both initial and ongoing formation for Catholic teachers.

A relevant, practical and affordable formation experience for Catholic teachers, I believe, is what we need during a time of economic scarcity in Catholic education. The model of formation I present in these pages can easily be implemented or adapted by Catholic educators who have good will, who are ready to be generous with some time, and who have a profound concern for both the present moment and future moments of Catholic education. It is my hope that this reflection on my own journey as a Catholic educator might prove to be helpful for other Catholic educators and an occasion for them to reflect on their own Catholic education journey—beginning or ongoing.

Part One
The Problem

**A reflection of a priest-educator
on the most critical issue facing
Catholic education**

I

Formation:
The Pressing Need

The real problem facing us in publicly funded Catholic education as we approach the millennium is the formation of Catholic educators. In Ontario, the defining moment for the urgent formation problem was full funding. In June 1984, then Premier William Davis announced in the Provincial Legislature at Queen's Park that the Government of Ontario intended to allow Ontario's Catholic high schools to become fully public. Until then, Roman Catholic separate schools received funding only to the end of Grade Ten. Funding through to Grade Thirteen or the Ontario Academic Credit (OAC) level meant immediate relief regarding the future viability of the schools.[1] Funding was accepted as a blessing. There was to be financial security. But even in June, 1984, some felt there was a curse dimension attached to full government funding: "The one who pays, controls!" Others were afraid of losing the charism and spirit of

---

[1]   "Full funding" is the term most often used to describe *Bill 30: An Act to Amend the Education Act*. Full funding for Catholic high schools is not, however, equal funding. Separate school trustees continue the struggle to have more just and equitable access to corporate assessment, the lion's share of which now goes to the public schools.

the private Catholic high school, developed and fostered over the years most often by religious communities of women an d men.

The Catholic High School Question

Extension of the separate school system through to Grade Thirteen—a blessing or a curse? Currently within Catholic education circles in Ontario, this question continues to be asked. Indeed, it is a healthy sign that the question remains, for it challenges teachers, trustees, administrators, parents, students and clergy to wrestle with the meaning of, and the very raison d'être for, a public Catholic school system. Bill 30 has occasioned a number of important reflections on the meaning and future direction of Catholic education in Ontario.[2] It is even more healthy when observers from outside the immediate Catholic education circles contribute to the debate. Such is the case when Kenneth Westhues, a professor of sociology at the University of

---

[2]   Among the more important studies:

• The Ontario Conference of Catholic Bishops, *This Moment of Promise* (Toronto, 1989).

• Institute for Catholic Education, *The Blishen Report: Catholic Education in the Separate School System of Ontario* (Toronto, 1990).

• Institute for Catholic Education, *Partners in Catholic Education Symposium III: After the Blishen Report* (Toronto, 1991).

•Institute for Catholic Education, *Catholic Education—Transforming Our World. A Canadian Perspective*, ed. Michael Higgins *et al.* (Ottawa: Novalis, 1991).

• James T. Mulligan, CSC, *Evangelization and the Catholic High School: Agenda for the 1990s* (Ottawa: Novalis, 1990).

• *Bridges to Faith: The Why and the How of High School Chaplaincy,* ed. Catherine M. Pead (Ottawa: Novalis, 1992).

• Ontario Separate School Trustees' Association, *The Philosophy of Catholic Education,* ed. Caroline F. DiGiovanni (Ottawa: Novalis, 1992).

• The Ontario Conference of Catholic Bishops, *Fulfilling the Promise: The Challenge of Leadership* (Toronto: 1993).

Waterloo, calls publicly-funded Catholic education "a curious inheritance" and "an ambiguous legacy."[3] Westhues argues that in contemporary Ontario, religion has dramatically diminished as a cultural priority. He sees a blanket of secularization—the standardization of cultural values—covering the Ontario spiritual and educational landscape. Religious and regional pluralism that used to give legitimacy to Catholic schools is no longer operative. Catholics and Protestants and "others" are now more alike than they are different.

> The result is that schools increasingly resemble one another. It is hard for any school to go its own way given the standardized culture the mass media instill in Canadian youth, and given constraint by a common set of provincial regulations and teachers' demands.[4]

Westhues questions sociologically the continued reasons for and place of a publicly funded Catholic separate school system in contemporary Ontario. His question should engage Catholic educators at all levels—trustees, administrators, teachers and parents—if the Catholic system is to be an alternative to the public school system.[5]

---

[3]   Kenneth Westhues, "Catholic Separate Schools: An Ambiguous Legacy," Grail, 1, 1 (March, 1985): 51.

[4]   Westhues, p. 57.

[5]   An "alternative system" or "schools with a difference" are ways Catholic educators often use to describe the purpose and approach of Catholic education. There is a danger that these descriptives smack of arrogance and elitism. For most Catholic educators with experience in "the trenches"—the classrooms, corridors and cafeterias of Catholic high schools—"alternative" does not mean "superior to" or "better than" the public high school. Rather, it means more "the ideal we strive for." "Alternative" finds its real meaning in the theology or philosophy at the foundation of Catholic school and Catholic board mission statements.

The 1984 full funding decision has, indeed, become "a moment of promise" in the words of the Ontario Conference of Catholic Bishops, but even more critically, a moment of serious and sober reflection so necessary if the promise of full funding is to be realized. In a challenging theological essay in *Compass,* Martin Royackers asks how graduates of Catholic high schools differ from graduates of public high schools in terms of moral values and the impact personal faith has on the social, political and economic dimensions of life.[6] He cites a 1979 study of civil servants who had been to Catholic schools which concluded: "personal faith plays no explicit part in the respondents' view of their work."[7] Kenneth Westhues' study concurs with this assessment:

> Research shows scant differences in moral values or achievement between graduates of tax-supported Catholic schools in Canada and graduates of public schools.[8]

Royackers challenges Catholic schools to become alternative schools. To do this, the Catholic high school must work: to present the Christ who transforms culture; to nurture and develop a critical faith; to hold as a high ideal graduates who will become agents of social change. Westhues, too, sees an activist role for Catholic schools if they are to have a raison d'être that will contribute significantly to the social and political life of Ontario. Catholic education must become a conduit for the social teaching of the Roman Catholic Church. Both Royackers and Westhues issue a bold, prophetic challenge to Catholic education

---

6   Martin Royackers, SJ, "New Identity in the Making—Catholic Schools Must Be Alternative Schools," *Compass,* October, 1988, pp. 23-24.

7   *Ibid.* Reference to E. Colin Campbell, SJ, *From the Ghetto to Ottawa: The Experience of the Catholic as Mandarin* (Regina: Campion College, 1979), p. 10.

8   Westhues, p. 57.

and to Catholic educators, a challenge that demands a serious renewal in the formation of teachers.

But are Catholic schools, and in particular, Catholic high schools, able to understand and then to accept this critical assessment and bold, prophetic challenge? This, I believe, is the fundamental question that faces the Catholic education community during these years of "promise." For me, this question has shaped and continues to shape my ministry as a Catholic educator.

A Pilgrimage in Ministry

My image of ministry is tied up with my image of church. I have a profound appreciation for the Vatican II image of pilgrim church. For me, my two-decade-long ministry as a Holy Cross priest-educator has been and continues to be a pilgrimage in faith. On this pilgrimage I have been engaged, questioned, challenged and enriched, both theologically and practically. In autobiographical fashion I briefly outline some of the theological moments that have impressed me and helped shape my present ministry as priest-teacher, as well as my present preoccupation in ministry.[9]

Some Key Moments of Personal Formation

I am a theological child of the Second Vatican Council. On December 8, 1965 I was standing in St. Peter's Square in Rome

---

[9]   I mean that I have been influenced and shaped by the more academic study of systematic and speculative theology and by the habit of ongoing theological reflection on my life and work as a minister: priest-teacher-preacher. I do not intend to develop here my theology of ministry or expand on some of my present theological and ministerial preoccupations. This I will do in Chapter 4. I feel it is important, though, at this point, to briefly share the significant moments/experiences that have influenced me as a practitioner of ministry.

for the concluding Eucharist of the Council. At the time, I was a first-year theology student at the Gregorian University. A few days before, the Bishops had given their approval to *Gaudium et Spes,* the Council's document on *The Church in the Modern World.* This document begins with these words:

> The joys and the hopes, the griefs and the anxieties of men and women of this age, especially those who are poor or in any way afflicted, these too are the joys and hopes, the griefs and anxieties of the followers of Christ.

And a few paragraphs later, the document continues:

> Inspired by no earthly ambition, the Church seeks but a solitary goal: to carry forward the work of Christ himself under the lead of the befriending Spirit.

> To carry out such a task, the Church has always had the duty of scrutinizing the signs of the times and of interpreting them in the light of the gospel. Thus in language intelligible to each generation, the Church can respond to the perennial questions which people ask about this present life and the life to come.... We must therefore recognize and understand the world in which we live, its expectations, its longings, and its often dramatic characteristics.[10]

The role of the church is to be in the world, to journey with men and women, to learn from the world, to interpret God's continued creative, redemptive and suffering presence in the world and to interpret the world to itself. The church's openness to and participation in the world, so present in this Vatican II ecclesiology, had a profound impact on my theological formation and my preparation for ministry. In the spirit and teaching

---

[10]   "Pastoral Constitution on the Church in the Modern World," *The Documents of Vatican II*, ed. Walter M. Abbott, SJ (London-Dublin: Geoffrey Chapman, 1966), Nos. 1 and 4.

of even these few lines of *The Church in the Modern World*, I have found some fundamental ideals for the mission of Catholic education. This is a first theological moment.

A second theological moment: it was an April afternoon in 1967, at the Gregorian University in Rome, that Lady Jackson, Barbara Ward, then editor of *The Economist*, lectured on *Populorum Progressio,* Pope Paul VI's encyclical *On the Development of Peoples.* Barbara Ward was a consultant to Pope Paul VI and assisted in the preparation of this document. Her lecture that day gave new meaning, credibility and urgency to Paul VI's encyclical. The encyclical became more than just an ecclesiastical document. For me this was a further development of the Vatican II openness and involvement in the world and an example of the dialogue that must take place between theology and the human sciences.

Evangelii Nuntiandi, Pope Paul VI's exhortation *On Evangelization in the Modern World* in 1975 made another significant contribution to my understanding of the ministry of Catholic education. This was a third theological moment. Again, in this biblically-inspired theology of Pope Paul VI, "the joys and griefs and anxieties" of men and women in the world are those, too, of the church, the followers of Jesus. The church is in the world and has as its task "to upset through the power of the Gospel" all that in the world is in contrast with the Word of God.[11] I was and continue to be very taken by the critical and prophetic dimension of Paul VI's theology of evangelization, which I will explain in some detail in Chapter 2.

Two further moments on my formative theological pilgrimage are worth noting, for they both serve to contextualize the critical theology that has shaped my understanding of and

---

[11]   Pope Paul VI, *On Evangelization in the Modern World (Evangelii Nuntiandi),* Rome, December 8, 1975, No. 19.

actions in ministry. On December 22, 1982, the Episcopal Commission for Social Affairs of the Canadian Conference of Catholic Bishops issued the statement, "Ethical Reflections on the Economic Crisis."[12] This document received banner headlines and front-page coverage in *The Toronto Star* on New Year's Eve, 1982. For me this document was critical theology entering squarely into Canadian social, economic and political life. It was, as well, an enshrinement in the life, action and teachings of the Canadian Roman Catholic Church of "the preferential option for the poor." The option for the poor was no longer a Latin American import: it was to be the priority in the way we evangelize in Canada. The contextualization of this critical theology has had an enormous influence on the way I understand Catholic education.

Pope John Paul II's visit to Edmonton on September 17, 1984 was a final theological moment that added both clarity and energy to my ministry as a Catholic educator. Reflecting in his homily on Matthew 25, John Paul II warned that we must not be content with an "individualistic" interpretation of Christian ethics. His theological anthropology—the human person lives in community—made it clear that there is a very demanding social dimension to Christian ethics. Thus, there will be a social dimension to judgement:

> Nevertheless, in the light of Christ's words, this poor South will judge the rich North. And the poor people and poor nations—poor in different ways, not only lacking food, but also deprived of freedom and other human rights—will

---

[12]   E. P. Sheridan, SJ, ed., *Do Justice! The Social Teaching of the Canadian Catholic Bishops* (Editions Paulines & the Jesuit Centre for Social Faith and Justice, 1987), p. 391. In April 1993, the bishops invited a new reflection on our present social and economic crisis in their letter, "Widespread Unemployment— A Call to Mobilize the Social Forces of the Nation."

judge those people who take these goods away from them, amassing to themselves the imperialistic monopoly of economic and political supremacy at the expense of others.[13]

Tracing these key moments in my theological pilgrimage underscores some of my foundational theological principles. It is this theology that has shaped and continues to shape my understanding of Catholic education and my practice as a Catholic educator.

Ministry in Catholic Education: A Personal Story

Let me continue autobiographically: I have been teaching in a Catholic high school founded by my religious community since 1969. In retrospect, I think of my ministry in the school in the 1970s as having been shaped by three different realities. There was, first of all, the overarching question of the financial viability of the school. This was the reality for most Catholic high schools in Ontario at that time. Although I was not an administrator of the school, as religious I shared in the worry and questioning and sacrifice so necessary to keep, as we would say, "the school afloat." I must remark here that this sense of responsibility and sacrifice was not just characteristic of the priests and sisters on staff. Lay teachers, parents and students also felt a certain ownership of the school, and while I don't want to idealize this reality too much, they were able to identify to various degrees with our community's charism of Catholic education.

Secondly, there was the overarching Vatican II context. The 1970s were post-conciliar years. It was a decade of radical change in the content and methods of doing religious education.

---

[13] Pope John Paul II, *Canada: Celebrating Our Faith* (St. Paul Editions, 1984), p. 273.

My teaching ministry had several concerns. First, curriculum and programs had to be created almost *ex nihilo*. The professional catechists of the time, in the national offices of religious education, were focusing on the elementary years. Given the natural rambunctiousness of adolescence and the post-Vietnam radicalism reflected in the music and youth culture of that era, no one, it seemed, was comfortable in producing religious education programs for secondary school students. Consequently, religion teachers had to produce their own program material and elaborate their own methods. Added to this was the fact that students were expected to take most of their religion classes without the reward of academic credits while they were earning credits for other subjects! These were definitely challenging years. But they were rich years, not unhappy years. I worked at creating courses, teaching these courses, and coaxing teachers with little or no background in religious education to teach these courses.

During this time, too, my Vatican II theology had thoroughly taken hold of me. It became increasingly obvious through the experience and practice of doing faith education with teenagers that the faith education, or rather, the underdeveloped nature of the faith education of their parents was even more problematic. The same observation could be made for the lay teachers on staff. Vatican II had called for renewal. There was an enormous challenge then for the renewal of adults, both teachers and parents. A small group of colleagues and confrères and I became a part-time adult education team in our high school to create a possibility for such renewal. It was largely faith education that we were concerned with, and throughout the 1970s we offered a variety of programs. This became an adjunct ministry to my full-time ministry as religion department head and teacher.

A passion for social justice and education for justice was the third factor at work influencing my ministry in the 1970s. In my own thinking, as I have already indicated, little by little the demands of *Gaudium et Spes* and *Populorum Progressio* became for me the rationale for a Catholic high school education in Ontario. If the awareness of the poor in the Third World and the challenge to work for change were not central in our curricular and co-curricular efforts, then we had no particular right or need to carry on. This was my thinking, shared by a few colleagues. It was by no means embraced by everyone at that time. It was this thinking, however, that governed the content of our religious education programs. The social justice component was central. Belonging to an international community of religious with confrères and classmates in Uganda, India, Bangladesh, Chile, Peru, Brazil and Mexico nurtured my own concern for Third World poverty and the global structures that maintain that poverty. Frequent visits by these confrères to our school made Third World persons and their problems more real. Co-curricular Starvathons and Pilgrimages for the Third World started at the school added spirit and political awareness and action to classroom learning for the students. The passion for justice has very much coloured my ministry.

In the 1980s, circumstances allowed me to integrate journeys to our Third World missions into my ministry of Catholic education. A sabbatical year in 1988-1989 was the occasion for me to reflect in a systematic way on the meaning of Catholic high school education. This reflection was occasioned by the implementation of extended government funding and the consequent proliferation of Catholic high schools across Ontario. As well, the challenging questions of critics like Kenneth Westhues, Martin Royackers and others fueled my thinking. My book, *Evangelization and the Catholic High School: Agenda for the 1990s*, was the fruit of this sabbatical year.[14] It was in researching and writing this book, and in the subsequent reflections occasioned by the book which I have shared with

---

[14]   James T. Mulligan, CSC, *Evangelization and the Catholic High School: Agenda for the 1990s* (Ottawa: Novalis, 1990).

concerned Catholic separate school educators across Canada, that I have come to identify what I feel to be the most pressing problem facing Catholic education: the formation—both initial and ongoing—of teachers.[15]

Unravelling the Problem

For a Roman Catholic religious, to teach in the Catholic high school in the 1960s and 1970s was to be engaged in the apostolate of Catholic education. For me during that time, teaching was not a job or even a profession. It was an important aspect of my vocation as a Holy Cross priest. My training or formation for this vocation took place in the universities, and in the novitiate and seminary of the Congregation of Holy Cross. For the lay teachers on staff at that time, teaching was a profession. But I believe that for many of them it was more than just a teaching job. In schools sponsored by religious communities, many lay teachers acquired the spirit of the religious community. They too had a sense of the vocation dimension of teaching in the Catholic high school. Hence, formally or informally, sometimes by osmosis more than anything else, there was a certain formational experience—lay teachers being immersed in and acquiring elements of the spirit and dedication of the religious community sponsoring the school.

The dramatic decrease in vocations to the religious life, and then full funding, which effectively removed control of the Catholic high school from the religious community and located it with the Catholic school board, have radically changed the situation for Catholic high schools. The formative experience once provided by religious to new lay staff is no longer present.

---

[15]   In Chapter 5 I elaborate in some detail my understanding of *formation*. For our purposes here, *formation* may be understood as the specific training or preparation needed to teach in a *Catholic* school.

Control on the part of a school board tends to centralize and bureaucratize. The community emphasis is diminished. The vision and philosophy that were part and parcel of the education charism of a religious community are rapidly disappearing in the Catholic high school.[16] There is a formation void.

A New Urgency

The necessity of formation, however, has never been more urgent. Publicly funded Roman Catholic education in Ontario defines itself as an alternative system to public education, an alternative with its philosophy or theology based on a Roman Catholic vision of education.[17] Essential features of that alternative vision are: possibilities for prayer and worship within the context of the school community; a curriculum that would reflect Christian Roman Catholic values and teaching; in-school pastoral care or chaplaincy; a vision of Catholic education that offers understanding and meaning rooted in the wisdom dimension of the Roman Catholic tradition and that issues the challenge and critique emanating from the prophetic dimension of the tradition; an understanding that to be a Catholic educator is to have a special vocation or ministry in the Roman Catholic church.

Church documents on Catholic education refer to the vocation of the Catholic educator.[18] Understood in this way, the

---

[16] This assessment was confirmed for me in my research for *Evangelization and the Catholic High School.* "Where is the formation?" "How are the evangelizers themselves evangelized?" Questions like these were posed time and time again by committed Catholic educators.

[17] This distinction can be found in the mission statements of Roman Catholic Separate School Boards. As well, in *This Moment of Promise*, the Ontario Catholic Bishops elaborate on the challenge of maintaining and deepening the Roman Catholic vision of education (pp. 20-22).

[18] See: *Lay Catholics in Schools: Witnesses to Faith* (Rome: Congregation for Catholic Education, 1982), paragraph 24.

teacher is called to serve in a special way (through the Catholic school and Catholic education) in furthering the mission of the church. But in the last few years, Catholic educators in North America are using the term "ministry" to describe faith education and faith animation with young people.[19] Increasingly, Catholic educators in Ontario are appropriating the term "ministry" to describe the role of the Catholic teacher. Here, the ministry of Catholic education is deemed to be an important element in the overall ministry of the Roman Catholic church in Ontario.

Catholic school board mission statements describe in lofty terms the vision of Catholic education, and church documents speak of the vocation of the Catholic educator. There are many problems, however, in translating the vision of Catholic education and the vocation of the Catholic educator into practice. While the ideals of publicly funded Catholic education in Ontario and elsewhere in Canada are well articulated, and while mission statements are produced and regularly reviewed, lived experience demonstrates in a telling way the lack of an adequate formation experience to prepare teachers to assume effectively their role as Catholic educators.[20]

Great Ideals . . . But the Practice?

To understand the difficulty in translating the ideals of Catholic education into practice, one must look first at the contemporary social, cultural and religious context. In 1956, I was a Grade Nine student at our Catholic high school. There were more than a dozen of our religious on the staff, four reli-

---

[19]   The respected American educator and theologian, Michael Warren, has pioneered the meaning and possibilities of youth ministry within the Roman Catholic tradition. See his: *Youth, Gospel, Liberation* (San Francisco: Harper & Row, 1987); and *Readings and Resources in Youth Ministry* (Winona, MN: Saint Mary's Press, 1987).

gious sisters and one lay man. Today there are three of our religious, one religious sister, and seventy-five lay women and men. Thirty years ago, 75 to 80% of Roman Catholics in Ontario were what one called "practicing Catholics"; that is, they went to Mass every Sunday. Today, depending upon location, only 15 to 30% "practice" their faith in a formal way. Thirty years ago, Catholics in Ontario had access to a system of shared symbols and values and meaning: sacramentals, devotions, family prayer, moral absolutes, holy days, consecrated bread and wine, a sense of sin, generally a sense of one's vocation in life as a Catholic. These symbols and shared meaning were knit together by regular Sunday practice on the part of families. Today's Catholic youth and young adults are too frequently growing up in an a religious environment with little or no contact with church life in the parish. Thirty years ago, there was socialization into what could be called for most Roman Catholics "the Catholic culture," and the Catholic school played a supporting role to the main actors: family and parish. Today, the Catholic church in Ontario

---

[20] One should distinguish here possible meanings of "Catholic educator":

• The Roman Catholic person teaching in a Catholic school;

• The Roman Catholic person teaching in a public or non-Roman Catholic school;

• The non-Catholic person teaching in a Catholic school.

My focus is primarily the first, the Roman Catholic teaching in the Catholic school. I am sensitive, however, to the contribution that non-Catholics can make in a Catholic school, especially in terms of commitment, respect for the Catholic difference and the attempt to live out the vision of Catholic education. I am aware, too, of their own peculiar formation needs for teaching in a Catholic school. My hunch is that the most effective formation experience for them would be to be a part of a group of Catholic teachers who are sincerely engaged in the struggle to do Catholic education and who see themselves as more than just professional educators by trying to live out the vocation of the Catholic educator. This would parallel the formation experience lay teachers received from religious when religious communities exercised such great influence in Catholic schools.

increasingly depends on the Catholic school to socialize students into the community of believers. The Ontario Bishops have correctly analyzed our contemporary Catholic experience and the critical role of the Catholic school in Catholic socialization:

> Within a society which is increasingly secular, there is more need than ever before for an educational community which stakes its existence on the infinite promise which Jesus Christ has offered through his death and resurrection. He came that we may have life and have it more abundantly.
>
> Given the increasing fragility of families and the overextension of parishes, it is becoming more obvious that the school, for some, is often the primary place where young people experience the Church as an alternative community which is shaped more by faith, hope and love than by the values of our consumer culture.[21]

Here the Bishops underscore the "secular society" and "consumer culture" factors that have so dramatically altered the religious landscape. The Catholic culture of thirty years ago is breaking down. Family life is being reshaped by forces beyond the control of the church: an economy based more and more on consumer materialism, the emancipation of women from fixed domestic roles defined by patriarchal values and radically different attitudes regarding sexuality. The family—the pillar of the Catholic culture of three decades ago—can no longer be counted on to be the lead actor in Catholic socialization.

The Bishops tend to gloss over the fundamental changes that have occurred in the second pillar of Catholic culture—the parish. They acknowledge that parishes are overextended. They

---

[21]   *This Moment of Promise* (Toronto: The Ontario Conference of Catholic Bishops, 1989), p. 16.

are silent as to the reasons. But the reasons are crucial, for they add to our understanding of the change taking place in contemporary Catholic experience. Parishes are overextended because of the influx of Catholic immigrants into Ontario since 1945; parishes are overextended because of the decrease in vocations to the priesthood; parishes are overextended because of an aging clergy (the average age is 66 years); parishes are overextended because of the theological poverty or timidity of a church leadership that does not seem to have the will or the creative imagination to fashion new structures that would meet the daunting pastoral challenges of our contemporary Catholic experience.

Consequently, as quoted above, the Bishops say: "It is becoming more obvious that the school, for some, is often the primary place where young people experience the church as an alternative community which is shaped more by faith, hope and love than by the values of our consumer culture." Three comments are in order here. First of all, I feel that the Bishops are being very conservative in their estimate: "for some." From my experience and from conversations with Catholic educators across the province, the Catholic school "for many" has become the primary place for young people to make contact with the church. Using the "practicing/non-practicing" classification of thirty years ago, the numbers are reversed. Now, perhaps 20 to 30% of the students would come from "practicing" families. For 70 to 80% of the students the Catholic school becomes first contact with and first experience of the church.

Secondly, the Bishops are really talking about the introductory experience or initiation into what it is to be Catholic today when they talk about the Catholic school as "the primary place where young people experience the Church." The school, then, for many is where Catholic socialization now takes place. This enormously important new ecclesial reality raises new questions for Catholic educators.[22]

Finally, this new ecclesial reality underscores the imperative for all in the Catholic education community to understand the privileged place the Catholic school can have in the mission and ministry of the Roman Catholic church.[23] I say "can have" advisedly, because so much depends on how serious Catholic educators take the challenge to translate the vision of mission statements into everyday practice; and how ready they are to embrace the demands, ideals and struggle that are part and parcel of the vocation of the Catholic educator.

Lack of Teacher Formation: A Huge Problem

While the new ecclesial reality underscores in bold strokes the challenges facing Catholic educators, it also uncovers the

---

[22]   Among the questions that acknowledgement of the new ecclesial reality (the Catholic school as the primary place where young people experience the church) raises are the following:
    • To what extent can the school take the place of parents in the socialization process into Catholic life?
    • What does it mean to be Catholic today? Are there degrees: e.g., churched Catholic / unchurched Catholic?
    • What elements of our Catholic heritage might be handed down through the Catholic school?
    • What strategies should the Catholic school community adopt in evangelizing (pre-evangelizing) the unchurched?
I will return to some of these questions in Part Three in the elaboration of a model of formation.
[23]   *The Religious Dimension of Education in a Catholic School* (Rome: The Congregation for Catholic Education, 1988), No. 33: "At least since the time of the Council, therefore, the Catholic school has had a clear identity, not only as a presence of the Church in society, but also as a genuine and proper instrument of the Church. It is a place of evangelization, of authentic apostolate and of pastoral action—not through complementary or parallel or extracurricular activity, but of its very nature: its work of educating the Christian person."

fundamental weakness in Catholic education today, and therefore its fundamental problem: the formation, preparation and readiness of teachers to translate a vision into reality and to live out a vocation. There is indeed a formation void. Presuming that only 30% of the Catholic population today consistently participates in the worshipping community, it can be extrapolated that the same would be true of an equal percentage of beginning teachers emerging from this same cultural and ecclesial context. But as we have seen, the vision of Catholic education and the understanding of the role of the Catholic educator demand so much more. The gap between what is real and what is expected is very problematic. There is a formation void.

The lack of teacher formation in Ontario is especially critical in the 1990s because of the rapid expansion (since 1985) of the separate school system, an expansion that has brought into the system many new teachers.[24] And in Alberta, the Alberta Catholic School Trustees recently hosted a two-day symposium on the question of teacher formation for the Catholic school. In his summary, "Synthesis and Commentary," Wilfrid Murchland, CSC, then President of Newman Theological College, remarked:

> Are our teachers prepared to teach in a Catholic school? A very impressive panel of new teachers, educated in the late 1980s, gave us a resounding "No!" to that question. The performance of the panel, one of the highlights of this symposium, will haunt those responsible for Catholic education in Alberta for at least the next decade and beyond. The clear conclusion is that what students received at home, in Sunday school, in elementary and high schools is an

---

[24] In my own research for *Evangelization and the Catholic High School* (Ottawa: Novalis, 1990), the lack of formation and the need for teacher formation were recurring themes. Chapter 12, "Evangelizing the Evangelizers," focuses in a particular way on the inadequacy of our present formation efforts.

insufficient base to teach in a Catholic school. Much more preparation at an adult theological level is required. "Winging it" is not an ideal but in all too many cases the reality.[25]

Here, too, in a system similar to Ontario's separate school system, there is great concern for the lack of teacher formation.

In July 1990, the Institute for Catholic Education released the research project, "Catholic Education in the Separate School System of Ontario," also called "The Blishen Report" after the director of the study, Professor Bernard Blishen. This study provides empirical data on how the Catholic adult population views separate school education, as well as data on the religious knowledge, attitudes and behaviours of a random group of Grade Twelve students in Catholic high schools. Judging by the reactions of the different partner groups in the Catholic education community, the data and findings of the Blishen Report are generally accepted as useful, but there is skepticism regarding some of the data and parts of the analysis.[26] The question of teacher formation is not raised directly in the Blishen Report. Two of the reaction papers to the Report, however, see teacher formation as a priority recommendation following from the Report. Hiring policies and the education of teachers in the faith were a concern for the clergy:

> The students need adults in the school who are good examples of living faith...; basically it will be up to the teachers. ...[W]e need to emphasize the vocation of Catholic educator.[27]

---

[25]   Wilfrid Murchland, CSC, "Symposium Summary and Wrapping Up Synthesis and Commentary," *Educating Teachers Symposium* (Alberta Catholic School Trustees' Association, 1990), p. 2.

The response of the Canadian Religious Conference-Ontario also highlighted the importance of teacher preparation. One respondent voiced this concern in a series of questions:

> What is done in our respective localities to evangelize teachers? What are the boards doing in this respect? The principals? What is done in Teachers' College to form our young Catholic teachers? Why not a Catholic Teachers' College? On what criteria are principals and superintendents chosen? Are they given adequate formation for their important role as Catholic leaders? Do the principals give Religion class its rightful place in the timetable? Are they preoccupied with the Catholicity of their school?[28]

It is my conviction that for the long-term viability and effectiveness of the separate school system, this question is the impor-

---

[26]   Refer to "Reaction Papers from Catholic Education Associations," the preparation document for *Partners in Catholic Education Symposium III: After the Blishen Report* (Toronto: Institute for Catholic Education, March, 1991). The reaction paper of the Ontario English Catholic Teachers' Association raises certain questions regarding the framing of the questionnaire for the student survey (p. 9). The philosophical premises at the foundation of the survey were seriously questioned by the Canadian Religious Conference-Ontario. Indeed, their paper suggests that because "the Report does not seem to reflect in its design the philosophy of Catholic education that is preoccupied with the whole person" (p. 21), it actually is a disservice to effective Catholic education." I continue to have difficulty with the survey's findings that 50% of students and 63% of parents and 87% of teachers attend Mass two or three times a month (p. 32). This data does not ring true with my own experience. These statistics seem to me to be inflated. I work with teachers; I teach students. I have been celebrating two Masses each Sunday in the same parish for the last three years. I know the students from the parish who attend the Catholic high school. I teach many of these students. I hold fast to my own assessment that only 20 to 30% of these students and their parents attend Mass each Sunday. I am confident that religion teachers in Catholic high schools across the province support my assessment.

[27]   *Ibid.,* p. 7.

[28]   *Ibid.,* p. 22.

tant one: "What is being done to evangelize teachers and to prepare teachers to teach in the Catholic school?"

A Proposed Model

There are valiant efforts to evangelize teachers in an ongoing way. Faith days, staff retreats, workshops on Catholicity across the curriculum, reflection groups on the meaning and effectiveness of the Catholic high school today all happen in Catholic high schools across the province. As to whether this type of continuing theological formation happens regularly and with great urgency in each school is quite another question. So much depends on the leadership of the principal of the Catholic high school. In some schools the bold and prophetic challenge of Kenneth Westhues and Martin Royackers to be an alternative school based on gospel values is taken with great seriousness. In other schools, the question is rarely posed. In-place school leadership in the person of the principal is key to the commitment to ongoing faith development of staff. It is my experience that the leadership of principals in this vital area is very uneven across the province.

For student teachers there is an optional religion course at faculties of education offered over two semesters. This is a course of ten to forty hours, depending on the faculty. The course is intended for student teachers considering applying for a position with a separate school board. Certainly, such a course is evidence that there is some progress in making the case in the faculties of education that a specialized preparation is necessary for student-teachers opting to teach in Catholic schools. But again, there is little that can be done philosophically, theologically and in terms of methods and strategies in such limited time, in a course student teachers carry over and above the standard course load at the faculty of education.

For beginning teachers and teachers already in the Catholic system in Ontario, there is "Religion: Part One." This course, sponsored jointly by the Ontario English Catholic Teachers' Association (OECTA) and the Ontario Separate School Trustees' Association (OSSTA) is approximately ninety hours in duration and is offered both in the summer and in evenings through the school year. While not universally mandated by boards, it is taken by most teachers now entering the separate school system. It consists of a general introduction to theology, scripture and liturgy with some valuable practical experience of strategies for teaching religion in the classroom as well as preparing and leading paraliturgies.[29] Over the last two decades "Religion: Part One" has been and continues to be a critically important formative experience. It is absolutely essential, but it is insufficient.

I say "insufficient," because we need more. "Religion: Part One" is introductory. It lays an important foundation that must be built upon. I am convinced that the task/ministry of the Catholic educator in the 1990s demands more: a more intense and ongoing formation; a more relevant and practical formation.

Given the challenge posed by both Kenneth Westhues and Martin Royackers to become an authentic alternative school system and because of the ideals wrapped up in the theological vision of Catholic education and the vocation of the Catholic teacher, teacher formation for the Catholic high school becomes an awesome task. Certainly, the new ecclesial reality that would place even more responsibility on the Catholic school only adds to the urgency and complexity of the task.

---

[29] This course has a Part Two and a Part Three. They are gradually more intensive in content but tend to be taken only by teachers specializing in religious education or seeking an administrative position in the separate school system.

Teacher formation for the Catholic school should touch on the fundamental ways of understanding and relevantly living out one's faith commitment to Jesus Christ as a teacher within the tradition of the Roman Catholic community. There are many options to chose from as attempts to provide both initial and ongoing formation. Given the importance of academic theology, it is clear that studies in biblical theology, Christology, ecclesiology, sacraments, ethics, liturgy, spirituality, catechesis, and social and cultural analysis are all necessary. It is in this area that "Religion: Part One" contributes invaluably.

But my focus for formation is more practical and more particular. In a practical way I believe that one's own experience as a Catholic educator should be the starting point for any formation or training. Consequently, I see formation taking place through a process of systematic reflection on experience and mutual sharing between beginning and experienced Catholic educators. In a particular way, I feel that this sharing or ongoing conversation between beginning teachers and committed, experienced teachers will be mutually enriching. It will allow the inexperienced teachers to encounter people who are committed to the serious task of translating ideals and convictions into action, and it will provide the experienced teachers with the opportunity to further reflect on their own experience and on the evolving demands of what it is to do Catholic education.

Finally, it is my conviction that the theology of evangelization elaborated by Paul VI in *On Evangelization in the Modern World* is a relevant and meaningful way of understanding the content and purpose of Catholic education today. I feel, too, that the changing social and ecclesial context increasingly demands that the teacher in the Catholic high school develop the spirit of and skills for interpretation, which I understand as the way a person goes about making sense of differing theologies, the way a person copes in an intellectual and social reality increasingly characterized more by plurality and ambiguity than by uniformity and certainty.

These are the essential elements in the model of formation I propose in Part Three of this book. The immediate task, however, is to develop my "understandings"—my theology of Church, ministry and evangelization; my notion of interpretation and how and why it is becoming so important for Catholic teachers; a more comprehensive look at the changing ecclesial context and Catholic culture; and my understanding and use of the category "formation" and how it functions in an adult learning experience. This task I take up in Part Two as I elaborate the theological, cultural and educational foundations for this model of formation.

Part Two

The Foundations for a Model of Formation

A reflection from a reading of the signs of the times

II

A Theological Reflection on Catholic Education

The formation of teachers—both initial and ongoing formation—to teach in a Catholic school is the most pressing problem facing Catholic education in the 1990s. Like their peers in public schools, Catholic educators are formed professionally in subject discipline and pedagogical methods at the universities and faculties of education. But for the Catholic educator, there must be something more if the teacher is to understand and embrace the vocation dimension of teaching in the Catholic school. The model of formation I describe in Part Three of this book is an attempt to propose a formation experience that can enable teachers to develop in the essential vocation dimension of teaching in the Catholic school. In the model of formation that I develop, however, there are some fundamentally important understandings—which I call *foundations*—that must be elaborated.

In this chapter I focus on two key theological understandings: ecclesiology—or an understanding of the church—and evangelization. In addressing the question of Catholic education, one must first of all explore the relationship between *Catholic* church and *Catholic* school and examine some of the ecclesiologies that are operative now in theologizing about Catholic education. I do this by critiquing an authoritarian model of church and proposing a model of church based on communion. And since my own bias is to look at the why and the how of Catholic education in terms of evangelization, there is a need to discuss the meaning of evangelization in the Catholic community today. I then develop some of the central elements of the theology of evangelization as I apply it to Catholic education.

A Reflection on the Church

Church and School

Catholic education is intimately connected with the mission of the Roman Catholic church. This is a given in official church documents on Catholic education. It is also a central element in the self-understanding of reflective Catholic educators.[1] In Chapter 1 I sketched some of the characteristics of a Roman Catholic vision of education: possibilities for prayer and worship within the context of the school community; a curriculum that reflects Christian Roman Catholic values and teaching; in-school pastoral care; a privileging of Roman Catholic social teaching; and an understanding that to teach in a Catholic school is to have a special vocation or ministry in the church. One sees here in practical ways how the mission of the church is manifest in the life and activity of the Catholic school.

---

[1] For the relationship between school and mission of the church see indicated passages in the following documents from The Congregation for Catholic Education: *The Catholic School* (1977), No. 9; *Lay Catholics in Schools: Witnesses to Faith* (1982), No. 12; and *The Religious Dimension of Education in a Catholic School* (1988), Nos. 31, 33, 34.

It is because of this intimate relationship that Catholic educators speak of "Catholicity" to describe how Catholic schools are different. Some schools have "Catholicity" committees to work at fostering the Catholic vision of education. There is, too, the "Catholicity across the curriculum" concern that is growing in importance in the curriculum offices at Catholic Education Centres across the province. Catholicity in the curriculum has as its purpose to show that teachable moments of Catholic theology and Christian values and perspective *do* exist in Ministry of Education courses that are not religion courses, and that to meet the challenge of the Catholic vision of education it is imperative that curriculum and faith education be not only related but integrated where appropriate.

> The teachings of the Church on the meaning of humanity, the development of peoples, ethical choices, and justice and peace, challenge Catholic schools to provide a critical transmission of the culture in the light of faith; to enable students to become active learners who understand both the process and product of learning; and to assist them in all aspects of personal growth. Curriculum and faith education are not separate elements in Catholic education. They can and must be interrelated. This interrelation affects how curriculum should be developed for Catholic schools. These schools are challenged to offer outstanding education in the context of gospel values which provide a vision of what it means to be a human being born in the image and likeness of God.[2]

For some, however, the term *Catholicity* smacks too much of an inquisitorial spirit. They prefer to speak of the *Catholic*

---

[2]   *Catholicity in the Curriculum: Curriculum Design Model Secondary Schools* (Mississauga, ON: Ontario Catholic Supervisory Officers' Association, 1991), p. 1.

character of the school.[3] A Catholic culture is a sacramental culture with a certain emphasis placed on signs and rituals that call to mind the immanence of God. Catholic education should reflect this culture. It is part of the Catholic character of education, as well, to privilege the questions of meaning:

> A Catholic school must be a place where all knowledge and relationships are transformed by questions of meaning, by the quest for meaning. We must have a profound respect for what is all too often repressed in this culture—that quiet voice which expresses the infinite desire of each person for God.[4]

The Catholic character will be reflected as well in management style; for example, modelling and promoting the servant-leader style of authority. Finally, Catholic social teaching should be prominently reflected in both the content and context of Catholic education: the subject matter taught and the atmosphere and relationships in which the teaching takes place.

Some Practical Concerns

This brief review of the vocabulary of Catholic education — Catholic vision of education — Catholicity — Catholicity across the curriculum — Catholic character of the school — demonstrates in an ideal way, or at least at the level of ideology, how the Catholic school participates in the mission of the Roman Catholic church. But a further question is the ecclesiological question. What is the understanding or understandings of "church" operative in the ideal descriptions of the mission of

---

[3]   I am indebted to Monsignor Dennis Murphy, the former Director of the Institute for Catholic Education in Toronto. In a keynote presentation he gave at the "Good News Challenge" Conference in Niagara Falls, Ontario on October 28, 1991, Monsignor Murphy elaborated his understanding of the Catholic character of the Catholic school system.

[4]   *This Moment of Promise,* p. 16.

Catholic education? Even more important is the ecclesiology question as it applies to the teachers, the main protagonists in the drama of Catholic education.

In the formation of teachers, the understanding of and attitude toward the church has several practical implications. Put in question form, a practical ecclesiology should address the following:

- What image of church nourishes teachers personally and gives them hope?

- How do teachers see themselves participating in the mission of the church?

- What image or understanding of church do they hand down to their students?

- What practices in the church cause concern for teachers, eroding credibility and leading to irrelevance — "a church out of touch!"

- What practices in the church build credibility?

- Granting that for many the school is where young people experience the church first, what are the implications of this new ecclesial reality for teachers in the Catholic school?

Ecclesiology is important and functions either in a reflective or non-reflective way in the practice of Catholic educators. My own intuition, shaped by conversations with teachers and other Catholic educators across Ontario, is that on the part of more than a few teachers there is a growing disillusionment with the *official church*. (By *official church* I understand *hierarchy*, when it is more authoritarian than enabling, *clergy* who are more cleric than servant, and outmoded, irrelevant *laws and disciplines* that are more obstacle than help.) At times, this disillusionment results in frustration and anger. My sense is that the more engaged the teachers are in the mission of the church and the

Catholic school and the more aware they are of the possibilities inherent in the ideals we hold and profess as church and Catholic school, the more frustrated and angry they become at official symbols and practices that only lead to the irrelevance and incredibility of the church.

A critical ecclesiology helps one understand the root causes of such tension, frustration and anger. At the same time, such an ecclesiology posits what *could be*, both at the level of understanding and of practice. I feel that the ecclesiologies of Rémi Parent and Leonardo Boff would help us to sort out and understand the practical ecclesiological concerns of Catholic educators outlined above.

A Critique of Clericalism

In *A Church of the Baptized*, Rémi Parent, a theologian at the University of Montreal, analyzes the clergy-laity relationship as it is presently understood and functioning in the church. His point of departure is his own experience of church as a theologian, but as a theologian sensitive to the anger, impatience, frustration and hurts of persons and communities "whose lay condition seems to prevent them living fully the church to which they nonetheless continue to cling almost desperately."[5] It is in this sense that I appreciate his critical theology of church and see it as a lens through which one might interpret the tension, frustration and anger of some Catholic educators.

Parent's thesis, fundamentally, is that the theology of Vatican II—of the documents *The Church, The Church in the Modern World* and *The Laity*—is often not being lived out. In still too many instances the laity are excluded from their rightful participation in the ecclesial community. In talking to Catholic

---

[5]   *Ibid.*, p. 1.

teachers across the country I can appreciate Rémi Parent's thesis. There are still some priests who operate from a position of power. Catholic teachers responsible for sacramental preparation, religious education and chaplaincy in our schools must deal with such clergy on a daily basis. Such experiences are painful. And it is precisely this painful experience of the laity, then, that is the *stuff* out of which Rémi Parent's ecclesiology emanates. A brief consideration of Rémi Parent's theology of the laity can help teachers understand with more clarity the theological reasons for some of the clergy-laity tension they may experience.

Historically the laity have come to know themselves in the church in terms of what they are not; that is, clerics. Parent cites the *Catéchisme de Poitiers* question:

> How do you know that you are members of the true Church? I know that I am a member of the true Church because I am united to my parish priest, and my parish priest is united to the bishop, who is himself united to the pope.[6]

It is only insofar as one relates to someone else in authority—priest, bishop, pope—that one knows oneself to be a member of the church. While Vatican II has superseded this archaic and distorted ecclesiology, Parent contends that in many instances the mentality and structure behind it are still in place, unfortunately. Too often there is a power theology paradigm still operative that continues to control. Clergy are leaders, laity are followers; clergy are at the top, laity at the bottom; clergy are knowledgeable subjects who promote and lead, the laity are objects passively accepting and following.

There is a pyramidal structure to the church which governs more than just the lay person's relations with the clergy. Rémi

---

6   *Ibid.,* pp. 22-23.

Parent believes that this top-to-bottom structure regulates our entire religious universe, our way of being church.[7] The following schema depicts this power paradigm. The laity are at the bottom, receiving.

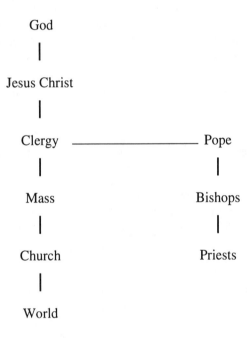

Parent concludes that to rethink the theology of the laity ultimately means to rethink the whole of theology: revelation, church, sacraments, orders, and even Christology.

Parent's analysis of our understanding or image of God illustrates how top-down, power theology functions. For the most part, he contends, Christians have a *theistic* notion of God. By this he means a notion of God as the one who created and

---

[7]   *Ibid.*, p. 28.

rules the universe and who is above; the one upon whom everything else depends. This very vision and idea of God renders believers passive: God is distant, transcendent, strange, without limits; we are here and now in history, dependent, and with limits. For Parent, theism is an ideology removing responsibility from the person.[8] As for clergy, the priests are of God: men of God, apart from the world (history) and attached to the sacred. Consequently, in our religious mentality they take on attributes of God: the leader, the decision-maker, the powerful one. The laity, on the other hand, are of the profane, the world. In classical theology, the world is where God is not! The world is to be avoided. It is the opposite of God. But this is the domain the laity have been given by the clergy.

Looking at Christology, Rémi Parent holds that the theistic vision has obtained.[9] In our religious mentality, the human Jesus is in submission to the divine Christ. The clergy, the priests, have appropriated for themselves the Christ of glory and the work of mediation — priest as *alter Christus* — while the laity are defined more by the incarnation: they are to work at the salvation of the world.[10]

Throughout his analysis, Rémi Parent recognizes and celebrates the radical changes in vocabulary and understanding occasioned by Vatican II, changes that should lead to different structures and empowerment of the laity. His fear, though, is that the power theology and pyramid structure are still very much in force.[11]

In our religious heritage, Rémi Parent notes that priests are understood as the mediators between God and people. This is so

---

[8]   *Ibid.*, p. 38.
[9]   *Ibid.*, p. 69.
[10] *Ibid.*, p. 73.
[11] *Ibid.*, p. 72.

especially because of their power to consecrate at Mass: "Thanks to their power over the Mass, the priests control, in effect, the coming of Jesus into history."[12] Parent sees this privilege of mediation giving to the priests total control over the process of production: dogmatic and moral discourse in the church; legislative, executive and judicial power in the church. In their relationship to priests, the laity are passive: they receive; they are given the life of Jesus Christ by the clergy. The laity have no power, no responsibility. The clergy dictate who may distribute communion and serve at the altar and who may reflect on the Word of God for the assembly. The laity continue to be defined as objects who receive, not as subjects who act and take responsibility.

In his analysis of the church, the key issue for Rémi Parent is unity. He remarks that unity as understood and practiced in the church today is "undifferentiated": it does not allow for differences. Clericalism imposes this one-dimensional unity or rather uniformity on the church. Because of their obsession with uniformity, the clergy must standardize. Consequently, Parent sees a sameness across the church globally, a sameness that is itself imposed from the top. Indeed, in the final analysis, the real question is how one understands revelation:

> God is not too disturbing as long as one pushes him up above or entrenches him behind a transcendence that isolates him from our lives. But answering to the logic of the Christian faith, what becomes of God as soon as one seeks him here below? What face does God take on when we respect the invitation of Jesus Christ and regard our lives, our personal and collective responsibilities, as the place of the revelation of God?[13]

---

12   *Ibid.,* p. 85.
13   *Ibid.,* p. 140.

For Parent, history dooms clerical uniformity. The Christian God is a God of history who continues to reveal himself in history. Experience shows that difference is essential to history, but difference is alien to standardization and clericalism. The real challenge for the church is to become a unity of plurality, a unity that embraces differences and otherness. He calls for an ecclesiological conversion, which means rejecting the uniformity of clericalism and its claim that unity has already been attained:

> I believe that the Church takes on meaning only in those for whom being Church is becoming Church. ... [T]his is indeed the challenge: to pass from a static cohesion based on the tranquil feeling of a possession of the truth to a communion given in such a way that the unity of the Church is always before us.[14]

In a word, Parent concludes from his analysis that the church must pass from the uniformity of the clerico-pyramidal church to the unity of plurality of the church of communion.[15] The church is always a church becoming.

Rémi Parent's theology is a synthetic theology that is relentless in its ability to make one question and re-think one's own Christology, ecclesiology and sacramental theology. He draws on his own mastery of these different theological disciplines, but at the same time he seems very much present to practice: to the parish, the chancery office, the conversations of people, the concerns and questions of Catholic educators. In a methodically systematic fashion he clarifies the problematic where clergy-laity tensions are played out.

---

[14]   *Ibid.,* p. 157.
[15]   *Ibid.,* p. 133.

While his synthesis is a strength, it can also be a weakness. I believe that it is not always as neat and schematic or black-and-white as Rémi Parent would have us believe. Considerable declergification or declericalization has taken place in the church since Vatican II. A closer look would reveal more than a little plurality and ambiguity at work now in the way the power/authority dimension of the church is defining itself. It is difficult to comprehend, as well, how patriarchy does not figure in the logic of his analysis. While his focus is on clergy-laity tension in the church, the feminist question is almost totally ignored. Surely, patriarchy figures prominently in the constitution of power theology and in the structures that continue to maintain that top-to-bottom control.

Yet I believe that Rémi Parent's diagnosis of the pathology of the church is a rich contribution to understanding the anger and frustration of some Catholic educators. His study shows that there is much more at stake than a sometimes tense personal clergy-laity relationship. The problem is fundamentally the structure, a structure based on power and control; a structure that deprives people of their subjectivity, or their responsibility to be and become church.

In his ecclesiological study, *Church: Charism and Power,* Leonardo Boff reaches a strikingly similar critique of the structural sickness of the institutional church:

> The system of power within the Church believes itself to come directly from God, and believers must accept it in faith. Socialization through catechesis, theology, and the accepted exercise of its power guarantees the preservation of the structure from generation to generation.[16]

---

[16]   Leonardo Boff, *Church: Charism and Power* (New York: Crossroads, 1985), p. 40.

While in his analysis Rémi Parent does pose challenges to the church and suggests possibilities for future movement towards the emancipation of the laity, his alternative ideal lacks the colours and the contours, the spirit and practical dynamics of Leonardo Boff's theology of the church. Boff contends that we must pass from a church of power to an alternative church, a church with charism as the organizing principle. It is this alternative church I will now briefly outline.

An Alternative Vision

The theology of conversion is Leonardo Boff's starting point and essential methodological principle as he analyzes the institutional church from the perspective of liberation theology. He is able to critique the structures sustaining the institution because of his deep conviction that "the Church is at the same time saint and sinner, always in need of conversion and reform."[17] Anchoring himself solidly in the auto-critical spirit of

---

[17]   *Ibid.,* p. 144. I should underscore here that it is precisely this humble dimension of Boff's theology that I find so attractive. I am aware that Boff's *Church: Charism and Power* raised certain doctrinal concerns for the Vatican's Congregation for the Doctrine of the Faith (CDF). In my brief discussion of Boff that follows I do not intend to enter into the polemic between Boff and the CDF. I see the Petrine office, the episcopacy and the Eucharist all as intrinsic to the church. I read Boff from a middle-class English Canadian perspective. I read Boff for the vision and hope his scholarship and experience offer me as a reflective practitioner. I embrace the idea and ideal of local church reborn in the ecclesiology of Vatican II. The challenge is to realize local church in my English Canadian reality, a reality quite different from Boff's Latin American context. I believe profoundly that the Holy Spirit is dynamically present in all believers and that all believers are called to evangelize. I agree with Boff and with popes and theologians through the ages that the church is always in need of reform— *ecclesia semper reformanda.* For me, Leonardo Boff renders an important service to the church in his analysis of ecclesial attitudes, structures and institutions in need of reform.

Vatican II's *Lumen Gentium* No. 8, Boff justifies his severe ecclesiological critique:

> I do not intend to denigrate the Church; this book presupposes an explicit adherence to the sacramental worth of the Church that must not only desire to affirm itself but also to foster self-criticism because "the Church ... is at the same time holy and always in need of being purified" (*L.G.*, No. 8). The credibility of its proclamation of human rights and its denunciation of their violations depends upon the respect that the Church itself practices.[18]

But conversion must be total and systemic. Institutional structures founded upon power must be analyzed in light of the gospel if authentic conversion is to take place. Leonardo Boff is suspicious, however, of the spirit and mode of conversion now operative among many exercising power in the contemporary Church:

> Vatican II explicitly stated the need for ongoing conversion in the notion of *Ecclesia semper reformanda* (Church always in need of reform). Unfortunately, conversion is interpreted in such a way that allows the power structure to remain as it is. An intimate and private meaning is given to conversion: the members of the Church must be converted; that is, live a morally holy life and achieve a purity of intentions. This does not touch upon the institution with its structures of ongoing iniquity, discrimination, lack of full participation, and so on. Institutions have a life of their own, independent of the good or ill intentions of individuals within them. If conversion does not reach the institution of the Church, if it does not call into question the way in which

---

[18] *Ibid.*, p. 33.

power is exercised, if it does not reach the wider society, then we cannot speak of gospel conversion.[19]

It is this personalist, privatized theology of conversion that is now proposed in too many seminaries and proclaimed in too many pulpits; conversion that is a critique of the institution as a corporate, systemic entity is regarded as being disloyal. For many laity, including Catholic educators, this failure to name and seek healing for the sins of the institution leads to further disillusionment with church leadership and reinforces the feeling that the church is incredible and, therefore, irrelevant. It is only from the theology of *Ecclesia semper reformanda* that a credible and relevant dialogue with the world and with "the joys and hopes, griefs and anxieties" of the people of our time can take place. If that spirit is absent in the deeds and actions of the church, all of our words are counter-productive.

Leonardo Boff, like Rémi Parent, argues that our failure in this regard is due to the fact that power rests in the minds and hands of a few specialists rather than being distributed throughout the entire community. The new model of church being born on the margins, in the *communidades ecclesiales de base* in Latin America, for example, is a community, a "*koinonia* of power." This "ecclesiogenesis", as Boff calls it, is a renunciation of the centralization of power but not a breaking away from the church of the apostles and tradition.

This new Church, as in all renewal movements, first appears on the periphery. Given the power structure at the center, the periphery is the only place where true creativity and freedom is possible.[20]

---

[19]   *Ibid.,* pp. 55-56.
[20]   *Ibid.,* p. 62.

The problem with the church of power is that it appears to be more absorbed in consolidating and protecting its institutional structures and reputation than it is with its mission, which is to be a sign of Christ for the world, and the place where the Spirit is explicitly active.[21]

A sign, Boff insists, does not exist for itself but for others, so the church as sign is a sacrament of the Holy Spirit, and it is in the Spirit that the Risen Christ continues to be present and active in history. Boff employs the wonderful image of chalice and wine to illustrate the sacramentality of the church:

> All of the institutions and theological language within the Church can and must be sacraments (signs and instruments) of the Spirit through which the risen Christ acts and is made present in the historical reality of all persons. If they are too rigid, and if they reject their function for faith and grace, they may become counter-signs of the Kingdom and of the presence of the Living Lord in the world. They must be like the chalice, serving the precious wine of the Spirit but not substituting for it, gathered in the humbleness of a human sign that it may be made present and tasted by all people.[22]

Aspects of Leonardo Boff's new church from the base resonate with many Catholic educators in English Canada who are unaware of ecclesiogenesis and who have scant knowledge of the existence and workings of Basic Christian Communities in Latin America.[23] While Boff notes fifteen different characteristics of the church born on the margins, I will highlight in summary form four of these characteristics that I believe strike a chord with reflective Catholic educators now ministering in the church in English Canada.

---

[21] *Ibid.*
[22] *Ibid.*, p. 153.

1. It is patently clear in Boff's ecclesiology that the church must be a church always conscious of its own need to be converted. This is the humility that gives credibility. It is the admission of vulnerability that makes the community of believers even more faith-full and hope-full about its need for the Spirit of the Risen Christ and its possibilities to be the chalice serving the precious wine of the Spirit—the liberating proclamation of the gospel.

2. The church is a church of the *laity* in the classical sense. Boff notes that *lay*, in its original Greek meaning, signifies a member of the *People of God*.[24] In this sense, priest, bishop and Pope are also *lay people*. As such, the church is the *koinonia* of power. Sacred power—the roles of leadership and coordination—is shared by the community.[25] In this way, then, the entire community is called upon to serve and minister.

3. The church is a church of the poor and dispossessed. Boff contends that it is especially in the poverty, desires and struggles of the poor that the church is most church. It is from the poor,

---

[23] In Chapter 8, "Characteristics of the Church in a Class Society," Boff is in agreement with Rémi Parent's thesis that within the church the clergy control the means of religious production. In the institutional church as it is presently constituted, there is a class society: those with power, those without; those who act and those who receive. The pathology in this reality is the concentration and exercise of power in the centre—the ruling class—thus rendering the others, the masses, powerless and passive. This classical Marxist critique of class structure certainly has legitimate application to church structures. Boff looks at the traditional notes of the church: one, holy, catholic and apostolic and applies this Marxist critique to illustrate how the clergy, those at the centre, control the means of religious production. The new model of church he then proposes in this chapter is a clever and appropriate twist of Robert Bellarmine's classical sixteenth-century tract on the church of the ruling classes.

[24] *Ibid.*, p. 118.

[25] *Ibid.*, p. 119.

and from Christ who continues to suffer in the poor, that the church derives the urgency of its mission.[26]

4.   Charism is the organizing principle of the church. Leonardo Boff, taking up Paul's notion of charism as the specific task that each person exercises in the community for the good of all,[27] reclaims the Pauline charismatic structure of the church:

> Charism was not just a privilege of the early days of the Church. It is the permanent condition of the Church as a community with diverse functions and services. Charism includes the hierarchical element, but not exclusively. Charism is more fundamental than the institution. Charism is the pneumatic force (*dynamis tou Theou*) that gives rise to institutions and keeps them alive. The principle of the structure of the Church is not the institution or the hierarchy but rather the charism that is at the root of all institutions and hierarchy. There is not one group of rulers and another group of those who are ruled; there is one group of faith. Those who rule as well as those who are ruled must all believe. Faith, or the charism of faith, is the *prius natura* [basic nature] and common factor giving rise to communication and fundamental fraternal equality among all members of the Church.[28]

In Boff's alternative church, each person is important, adding to the community of faith and co-constituting the Church.

There are many today in English Canada who express similar ideals for the church and ideas about the church. Some of these are Catholic educators who know little or nothing of Leonardo Boff and Rémi Parent and their ecclesiologies. Their sense

---

[26]   *Ibid.*, p. 10.

[27]   *Ibid.*, p. 157.

[28]   *Ibid.*, pp. 159-160.

of church—of a humble church, a servant church, a church that is a people on pilgrimage with a special love of and preference for the poor, a church that empowers people, recognizing gifts and encouraging their use—has been fashioned gradually through living out of the theology and the spirit of Vatican II over the last quarter century. This is the type of church that has been celebrated in homilies and hymns, liturgies and retreat experiences. It will not easily be surrendered, since too many lay people have claimed ownership of the mission of the church and of ministry within the church. Through theological critique and retrieval of the communal ideals of the primitive church, Rémi Parent and Leonardo Boff propose an ecclesiology very much in the spirit of Vatican II; an ecclesiology that articulates the notions and yearnings of some Catholic educators.

A Reflection on Evangelization

Evangelization is the second theological understanding that must be clarified. I have stated that my own bias is to understand and engage in Catholic education as evangelization. But what exactly does this mean? Evangelization is a term that evokes many meanings and understandings, and in the Catholic tradition it is a term that has only recently attained acceptance as a theological descriptive for the mission of the church. According to American ecclesiologist Avery Dulles, Karl Barth and other Protestant kerygmatic theologians had considerable influence on Catholic European theology in the 1940s and 1950s.[29] The imperative for the Christian church facing a de-Christianized Europe was to proclaim with confidence the basic message of salvation through Jesus Christ.[30] Inspired by kerygmatic

---

[29]   Avery Dulles, SJ, "John Paul II and the New Evangelization," *America* (February 1, 1992), p. 52.

[30]   *Ibid.*

theology, the Catholic catechetical movement began to look at Christian initiation in three distinct stages: pre-evangelization was concerned with arousing interest in faith questions in people; evangelization was the proclamation of salvation in Jesus Christ; and finally, catechesis had to do with faith instruction before initiation into the sacraments.[31]

Dulles notes that Vatican I (1870) used the word *gospel* (*evangelium*) only once. By 1965, "gospel" and doing and proclaiming the gospel or "evangelization" had penetrated deeply into the formal Catholic consciousness:

> Vatican II, by contrast, mentioned the "Gospel" 157 times, "evangelize" 18 times and "evangelization" 31 times. When it spoke of evangelizing, Vatican II seems generally to have meant what the kerygmatic theologians meant by the term: the proclamation of the basic Christian message to those who did not yet believe in Christ.[32]

But evangelization as a term and as a dynamic way of conceiving the mission of the Christian community today has not had as easy a time seeping into the consciousness of ordinary Catholics. For many Catholics, "evangelization" is something Protestant. The crusades and television programming of some fundamentalist preachers have not helped. Many Catholic educators associate the term with "televangelism" and the Swaggarts and Bakkers of Sunday morning television. The ethical short-comings and crass entrepreneurial focus of some of these "evangelists" only add to the Catholic suspicion of any word that sounds like evangelization.

---

[31] *Ibid.*, p. 53.
[32] *Ibid.*

The Theology of Evangelization of Paul VI and Catholic Education

In Chapter 1 I remarked that I was very taken with *Evangelii Nuntiandi,* Pope Paul VI's 1975 apostolic exhortation, *On Evangelization in the Modern World.* In appropriating Pope Paul VI's theology of evangelization and applying it to what goes on in Catholic education in Ontario, I am very much struck by the way Paul VI roots the evangelizing mission of the church in the evangelizing mission of Jesus. I have already indicated that I believe that the Catholic school, in a very fundamental way, is about proclaiming the good news of Jesus Christ. Now, to elaborate this thesis, I will present what I believe to be six critical principles of Paul VI's *On Evangelization in the Modern World.* In addition, I will show how they constitute the framework for a relevant and appropriate theology of Catholic education for the 1990s.[33]

1.   *The mission of the Church is to evangelize.*

> The Church exists in order to evangelize; this is the vocation proper to the Church (*E.N.* 14). The Church is born of the evangelizing activity of Jesus and the Twelve; it is above all Jesus' mission and Jesus' condition of being an evangelizer that the Church is called upon to continue (*E.N.* 15).

The evangelizing mission of Catholic education and the vocation of the Catholic educator to evangelize, then, are grounded solidly in the evangelizing mission of the church.

---

[33]   In this outline of the six critical principles, I paraphrase and condense the passages cited from *On Evangelization in the Modern World*, identifying them with *E.N.* and the paragraph number.

2. The whole Church receives the mission to evangelize.

Thus it is the whole Church that receives the mission to evangelize, and the work of each individual member is important for the whole (*E.N.* 15).

The evangelizing mission is diffused throughout the community. Gifts and talents are likewise richly distributed. The work of every person advances the mission. In this passage Paul VI invites us for a brief moment into a declericalized community, the *laos* in the classical sense of the term used by Leonardo Boff, a people using gifts and encouraging the use of gifts for the proclamation of the Good News. This ideal of a mission-ed, empower-ed people is most applicable to the Catholic education reality in Ontario in the 1990s. The new ecclesial reality is that the Catholic school for many is the primary place where young people will encounter Jesus and his teaching, and it is Catholic educators, the laity, who are the evangelizers.

3. Evangelization proceeds from humility and the felt need to be evangelized.

The Church is an evangelizer but begins by being evangelized itself. The Church is the community of believers, the community of hope lived and communicated, the community of mutual love, but it must always listen to what it must believe, to its reasons for hoping, to the new commandment of love. The Church is the People of God immersed in the world and often tempted by idols, and it always needs to hear anew the proclamation of the Good News which converted it to the Lord. The Church has a constant need of being evangelized if it wishes to retain freshness, vigour and strength in order to proclaim the Gospel with credibility (*E.N.* 15).

For me this is the heart of Paul VI's theology of evangelization. This is evangelization from brokenness, from weakness. It

is a going out to the world fully aware that we need the Good
News even more than the world if we are to be credible. This is
humble theology from Paul VI that invites critique, analysis and
feedback about the effectiveness or oppressiveness of the
systems, structures and strategies of the institutional church. I
find Paul VI's reflections on the content, spirit and methods of
evangelization all the more credible because they are grounded
in the acknowledgement of the church's own sinful condition
and constant need to be evangelized. I am convinced that Paul
VI's invitation to self-critique is applicable to the Catholic
teacher, to the Catholic school staff or community, to a Catholic
school board or system, and must always be the starting point for
every life review or revisioning process. As Catholic educators,
personally and corporately, we are evangelizers, but we must
begin, personally and corporately, by being evangelized
ourselves.

4.   *Evangelization has a transforming and critical quality.*

For the Church, evangelizing means to bring the Good
News into all the strata of humanity, and through its influence, to transform humanity from within and make it new.
The purpose of evangelization may be expressed in one
sentence: the Church evangelizes when it seeks to convert,
solely through the divine power of the message it proclaims,
both the personal and collective consciences of people, the
activities in which they engage, and the lives and concrete
milieu which are theirs (*E.N.* 18). For the Church it is not
only to preach the gospel more widely geographically or to
greater numbers of people, but also of affecting and, as it
were, upsetting, through the power of the gospel, humankind's criteria of judgement, points of interest, determining
values, lines of thought, sources of inspiration and models
of life, which are in contrast with the gospel and the plan of
salvation (*E.N.* 19).

There is no dualism—sacred sphere and secular sphere—in Paul VI's theology of evangelization. It is an integral evangelization that confronts all aspects of life: political, economic, social and cultural. That is why I find this theology so appropriate to describe the nature and purpose of Catholic education. Indeed, there is no neutral subject or discipline. The gospel perspective is the lens through which Catholic educators and students together investigate and analyze all values and actions, attitudes and relationships. And it is an upsetting gospel that must often be proclaimed. This resonates with Leonardo Boff's "living presence and dangerous memory of Jesus Christ"! To challenge and at times upset humankind's criteria of judgement, points of interest, lines of thought and models of life with the memory of Jesus' actions and teaching will necessarily be a risky and even dangerous vocation. It is precisely this transforming, critical evangelization that is at the core of the church's social teaching, a social teaching that Ken Westhues and Martin Royackers see as legitimating Catholic education and Catholic schools. To be the conduit of the church's social teaching, to propose a critical education with the purpose of transforming society—this is an authentic and credible raison d'être for Catholic education. Unfortunately, it is my experience that this critical principle of Paul VI's theology of evangelization, if it is considered at all by schools and educators, remains mostly at the level of ideal in Catholic high schools across Ontario. As I have stressed in Chapter 1, the transforming, critical quality of evangelization is the foundational theological principle of my own vision of Catholic education, an ideal that I constantly struggle to put into practice.

5. *Witness of life is of primary importance in evangelization.*

Above all, the gospel must be proclaimed by witness (*E.N.* 21). It is important to recall the following: to evangelize is first of all to bear witness, in a simple and direct way, to God revealed by Jesus Christ, in the Holy Spirit; to bear witness that in his Son God has loved the world; that in his Incarnate Word he has given being to all things and has called all to eternal life (*E.N.* 26). For the Church, the first means of evangelization is the witness of authentically Christian life: modern men and women listen more willingly to witnesses than to teachers, and if they do listen to teachers, it is because they are witnesses (*E.N.* 41).

I privilege proclamation of witness over the proclamation of the Word because I am adapting Paul VI's theology of evangelization to the concrete situation of Catholic education.[34] Any experienced parent or high school teacher will say: "Young people do not like to be preached at." "Walk your talk" is the jargon often heard today, with more than a little truth in it. The witness dimension of evangelization is the most effective method in the Catholic high school. Most high school teachers are not theologians. Most of them have little training in catechetics. But they are adults, and given the Catholic education context, it is only right that they be expected to work towards achieving an adult ownership of their faith. (Certainly adult ownership of faith and commitment to Jesus is the ideal, but it also constitutes the challenge and the struggle of initial and ongoing formation.) Catholic educators are questioned by this invitation of Paul VI to witness: "What about your style of

---

[34]   There are very definite proclamation moments in the life-cycle of a Catholic high school education. Paul VI is adamant that the Good News proclaimed by the witness of life must sooner or later be proclaimed by the word of life: there is no true evangelization if the name of Jesus and the Kingdom of Jesus are not proclaimed in word (*E.N.* 22). These proclamation moments, however, are more infrequent. Witnessing is the everyday challenge. But pastoral counselling, small group liturgies, retreat days, school Eucharist, reconciliation services and graced moments of personal story-telling (without being "churchy") on the part of a Catholic educator, all constitute moments of the proclamation of the word.

teaching . . . your rapport with students . . . the ways you reveal your own life priorities and values? Does your wordless witness go very far in helping students discover a little more about meaning in their own lives and the important questions they should address on their own journey through life?"

6. *There is a need to adapt evangelization.*

Individual churches have the task of assimilating the essence of the Gospel and of transposing it into the language of a particular people and then of proclaiming it in this language. *Language* is understood in a cultural way. Evangelization loses much of its force and effectiveness if it does not take into consideration the actual people to whom it is addressed, their language, signs and symbols; if it does not answer the questions they ask; and if it does not have an impact on their concrete life (*E.N. 63*).

For any school community, the first task in the education process is to know the students. What does a social analysis indicate? What are the economic, cultural and ethnic conditions of the neighbourhood? The point is that we begin education where the students are, not where we would like them to be. The content, methods and processes of education will be conditioned by the background of the students. Education must be adapted. In Catholic schools, this same adaptation must characterize our evangelization. What is the faith background of our students? Churched or unchurched? Does the local parish contribute to the evangelizing efforts of the school, or is it an obstacle? What are the questions of the students, their signs and symbols? As we shall see in the following chapter, interpretation or discernment is the invaluable skill and attitude needed if we are to adapt evangelization to address the vital questions and needs of students.

I select these six elements from the theology of evangelization of Paul VI because I feel they constitute the framework for elaborating the purpose and fundamental content of Catholic education. There are other philosophies of Catholic education; there are other ways of visioning Catholic education. None, however, in my opinion, is as relevant or appropriate as this bold, challenging theology of evangelization. *On Evangelization in the Modern World* proposes the content of evangelization, but at the same time it is relentless in its challenge that the evangelizers live what they witness and proclaim.

III

A Conversation with Culture: A Must!

Traditionally, Catholic education has been looked at as the *traditio fidei*—the handing down of the faith. To hand down the faith in our time, however, within institutional structures such as dioceses, parishes, and schools, is no easy matter. It becomes even more complicated when one considers the culture in which all of this takes place. A conversation with culture is necessary, so, equipped with some philosophical, sociological and psychological modes of analysis, I will engage in this chapter in a dialogue with culture by investigating four aspects of what I call our present "Catholic crisis": the crisis of meaning, the crisis of authority, the crisis of modernity and the crisis of understanding. Such a dialogue with culture is beneficial because, along with achieving a deeper understanding of some of the root causes of the present Catholic malaise, one uncovers as well seeds of hope within the tradition. One finds as well new approaches (which are really old approaches) to evangelization: the rediscovery of the Catholic principle of sacramentality, and the adoption of a hermeneutical stance (the imperative for the Catholic educator today to be an interpreter of social and ecclesial reality). I will look at the meaning of sacramentality and interpretation and outline how both of these theological realities can enrich evangelizing efforts in Catholic education.

The Challenge to Interpret the Tradition in Dialogue with Contemporary Catholic Culture

As we look at Catholic education from the point of view of ecclesiology, it becomes clear that we must also explore the lived reality or the cultural dimension of what it is to be a Roman Catholic and a Roman Catholic educator in Ontario in the 1990s. There are different ways of understanding church. There are, as well, different conceptions of the mission of the church. And there are, necessarily, different ways of being church and living out one's membership in or affiliation with the church. There is, I believe, a Catholic culture in English Canada, and this culture is constituted largely by the various ways Roman Catholics belong to the Roman Catholic church and the different meanings they derive from membership in that church.[1]

But in the last quarter-century, this culture—these symbols, institutions and systems of meaning that have so structured the

---

[1]   Mary Jo Leddy defines culture as that all-pervasive reality of the symbols, institution and systems of meaning that structure not only our society but our inner selves as well. See: Leddy's Reweaving Religious Life (Mystic, Connecticut: Twenty-Third Publications, 1990), p. 21. For Bernard Lonergan, culture is "a set of meanings and values informing a common way of life, and there are as many cultures as there are distinct sets of such meanings and values." This definition is from Lonergan's Method in Theology (London: Carton, Longman & Todd, 1972), p. 301, and is quoted by Charles Davis in his essay, "Vatican II and Catholic Culture," The Ecumenist, (Spring, 1991), p. 14. I like John Coleman's image of culture as a map providing us with the data of who we are, where we have come from, where we need to go together in his "Culture at the Core of our Being," Compass (January/February, 1992), p. 5. I believe Coleman's image accurately describes pre-Vatican II Catholic culture. At the same time, I find it challenging for the post-Vatican II culture to chart the central thoroughfares of symbol and meaning that brought us to where we are now. It is in these routes of meaning from the past that we will find direction for the future. Throughout this discussion, I restrict my analysis of Catholic culture to the English Canadian Catholic reality.

way Roman Catholics view the world and relate to the world—
has been and continues to be significantly reshaped. What has
happened? What are some of the critical ideological forces operative in this reshaping? What is it in Catholic culture that is
helpful for the journey into the future? These are the questions I
will now address.

Before 1965, there were clear and quite definite characteristics of what it was to be a Catholic. Catholic culture was easily
defined. Most Catholics were practicing Catholics; that is, 75 to
80% of Catholics were at Mass every Sunday. There was an
authority structure in place, and it was religiously followed.
Catholics in English Canada at that time had access to a system
of shared symbols and values and meaning: sacramentals, devotions, family prayer, moral absolutes, holy days, consecrated
bread and wine, a sense of sin, and generally, a sense of one's
vocation in life as a Catholic. These symbols and shared
meaning were knit together by a strong attachment to parish
community and a home life that reflected Catholic meaning and
values. Catholics at that time shared a "Catholic world view",
well ordered, with clearly defined absolutes and very little ambiguity.

Since 1965 and the end of the Second Vatican Council,
however, the ways Roman Catholics understand themselves as
members of the church have changed dramatically. Catholic
culture in English Canada is no longer easily defined. Liberal
and conservative, churched and unchurched, progressives and
traditionalists, pro-life and pro-choice: it would appear that there
are several Catholic churches in Ontario in the 1990s, and
perhaps even several distinct Catholic cultures.[2] As was noted in
Chapter 1, Sunday Mass attendance has dropped from 75 to 80%

---

[2]   Using Lonergan's definition of culture, there may, indeed, be several
Catholic cultures or sub-cultures operative in English Canadian Catholic life,
since there now seems to be a plurality of sets of meaning and values informing
different groups of believers who identify themselves as Catholic.

to 20 to 30%; attitudes toward church authority, especially teaching on sexuality, have changed radically. (Many Catholics practice artificial birth control and seem indifferent to the church's doctrine on sexual morality.) There is an increasing fragility to home life. (The Ontario Bishops, as we have seen, have underscored the fact that it is the school, more and more, that teaches children how to pray; it is the school that is often the first point of contact children have with the church.) And there is a certain disillusionment on the part of a growing number of Catholics with a segment of the decision-making leadership of the church which continues to promote stifling patriarchal values by its words and deeds. This is by no means an exhaustive list, but these are some significant elements of the lived reality of what it is to be Roman Catholic in the 1990s.

Some commentators have referred to contemporary North American Catholic culture as a culture in crisis. Yet, it is precisely this culture in crisis that Catholic educators live in and work in and that they are expected to understand as they participate in the mission of the church that is Catholic education. Space does not permit more than a cursory examination of a few of the fundamental ideological forces shaping and reshaping this Catholic culture in crisis, an examination that is, nonetheless, critically important if one is to appreciate the challenge facing Catholic education to make the gospel real and relevant and to interpret the profound wealth of Catholic tradition[3] to the Catholic teachers and students in our ever-changing ecclesial reality.

---

3   In the April 18, 1992 issue of *America*, Richard McCormick underlines the dynamic nature of *tradition*: "In a real sense, then, tradition is always in transition. To think otherwise is to confuse tradition (the living faith of the dead) with traditionalism (the dead faith of the living)," "Moral Theology in the Year 2000: Tradition in Transition", p. 312. By *tradition*, then, I mean here the living faith of the dead, the understandings, symbols, rituals and outlook that have been handed down to us in our Roman Catholic heritage and that continue to nurture us with meaning and give us a sense of direction. In nurturing us, the tradition in turn evolves and is itself reshaped by our living it.

Catholic Culture in Crisis: An Overview

It is instructive to attend to a critical analysis of contemporary Catholic culture. In their studies touching on aspects of the life and activities within the Roman Catholic church, different observers can help us understand how our present crisis has evolved, and this understanding, in turn, can be useful in devising appropriate evangelizing strategies—charting new routes of meaning for the future. At the very least, understanding some of the background of the crisis can make coping with it a little less stressful.

The Crisis of Meaning: Searching for a Common Vision

Mary Jo Leddy suggests that the liberal and conservative factions in the church reflect the broader social context of the liberal and conservative experience of living contemporary North American economic and political life.[4] She argues that it is the absence of a common vision or a sense of meaning that is at the heart of the crisis of North American culture. The conservative response to the chaos and confusion experienced because of the lack of a shared vision in society today is to return to the past to retrieve the law and order and value system that worked then. While supportive of the conservative instinct for a more profound, common sense of purpose and meaning, Mary Jo Leddy doubts that the conservative approach can be successful, for two reasons. In the first place, such a common vision would be imposed by the conservatives. This coercive use of power is contradictory in a free, democratic society. Secondly, the present decline in North American culture is due in large part to free-market, conservative economics, which itself is the cause for the erosion of the traditional conservative base of home, family and small business. Indeed, Mary Jo Leddy notes that free-market

---

[4]   See Leddy, *Reweaving Religious Life* and her essay, "The Meaning of Catholic Education in a Post-Liberal Age," in the Institute for Catholic Education's *Catholic Education: Transforming Our World* (Ottawa: Novalis, 1991).

economic policies of the 1980s have bitterly divided society by widening the gap between rich and poor.

The liberal experience and way of coping in the present-day cultural crisis is rooted in the philosophy of liberalism.

> Liberalism saw the free market as an interaction of conflicting individual interests that would eventually produce the greatest good for the greatest number of people. Liberalism did not then, and does not now, begin with an integrating vision of the whole, but rather, with the assumption that the individual is the starting point in economic, political and social arrangements. Liberalism believes that the common good will result from the self-actualization of each part.[5]

Thus, while liberals promote individual rights and personal development, they are inherently suspicious of any attempt to impose a common program or moral order on society.

For Mary Jo Leddy, Catholic conservatives reflect the broader, cultural conservative agenda. They regret the modernizing experience of Vatican II, holding that it was nothing but accommodation with secularization. Before Vatican II there was a central, broadly accepted Catholic vision that managed to stand over and against the culture. But not any more! The Catholic conservative response, like the broader conservative response in the political arena, is coercive; it seeks to re-impose order, to discipline, to restrict the use of power in the church to the hierarchy. All of these strategies are proving to be as alienating and ineffective in the church as Christian community, as the more global, conservative, social and economic strategies are in society.

---

[5]   Leddy, *Reweaving Religious Life*, p. 36.

But liberals, on the other hand, while promoting freedom, democratic structures, and human rights in the church, are still insensitive to the deep human desire for a common vision:

> Catholic liberals are wary of the traditional calls to sacrifice and commitment. Although they are critical of conservative tendencies in the church, they tend to be less critical of the liberal culture. As a result, they become more vulnerable to the generalized trend toward economic selfishness, the psychologies and spiritualities of self-development. Thus, the liberal option in the church ultimately mirrors another pattern of decline within the culture.[6]

Holding fast to their respective ideologies, conservatives and liberals within the church might find support and therapeutic comfort in like-minded allies, but they fail to contribute in any significant way to resolving the crisis of meaning in Catholic culture today. On the contrary, they seem only to add to the malaise, spending time and creative energy defending their own theological and ecclesiastical turf and attacking that of their opponents, when so much of that same time and energy is called for to work at the fundamental problem of common vision within the church today.

The Crisis of Authority

The crisis in American Catholicism really has to do with a crisis of leadership in the church. The laity in the United States have cut back on financial contributions to the church because of their anger at and frustration with a clerical leadership, seemingly out of touch with the lived reality of American Catholics. This is the view of American sociologist, Andrew Greeley, in his

---

[6]   *Ibid.*, p. 51.

study of the behaviour and beliefs of American Catholics.[7]
While Greeley's empirical data measures the American Catholic
experience, I feel that much of it would apply to the English
Canadian reality. I believe this to be the case especially with the
encyclical *Humanae Vitae* (1968) and its impact on the laity.
Greeley contends that this encyclical and the reaction to it is the
most important event in the last twenty-five years of church
history:

> In their response to the encyclical, many of the most devout
> Catholic laity (especially of Irish and Polish background)
> for the first time deliberately disobeyed the pope. The fact
> that they did so and were not greatly troubled afterwards
> prepared them for a future in which increasingly they would
> make their own decisions on moral and religious matters
> and yet continue to participate as active Catholics.[8]

For Greeley, the encyclical occasioned an experience of
emancipation for the Catholic laity, especially in sexual matters.
The authority of the church came to be ignored by the laity; and
what is more, it was immeasurably tarnished and deemed irrelevant to their own experience of sexuality, intimacy and marriage.
In addition to this rejection of authority on the part of the laity,
the encyclical had a terribly demoralizing influence on many
clergy and religious. The leadership of the church had lost credibility and for many clergy, especially those caught up in the
renewal of Vatican II, a malaise, a crisis in morale set in, that still
exists today.

While Greeley studies American culture as a sociologist and
builds his case with sociological data, Eugene Kennedy investigates the psychology of being an American Catholic in his study,

---

[7]   Andrew M. Greeley, *The Catholic Myth* (New York: Collier Books,
1990).

[8]   *Ibid.,* p. 91.

The Now And Future Church.[9] For Kennedy, too, the crisis in Catholic culture is a crisis of authority, but unlike Greeley, who pinpoints the 1968 *Humanae Vitae* encyclical as the crucial moment, Kennedy sees the coming of age of an immigrant church, from being a strict hierarchical-authoritarian church to being a responsible and co-responsible community, a collegial church, as the moment of transformation. Kennedy's American church was basically an immigrant church which found social identification with the rigid discipline and doctrine of the church. This 19th and early 20th-century church was a church marked by what were considered to be the primary virtues of duty, loyalty and obedience:

> The vocational supply of this church was dependent on an obsessive-compulsive social structure that was held in place, as long as it lasted, by authority that often expressed itself as authoritarianism. This was essentially a hierarchical culture . . . . [10]

But in the first half of the 20th century, Kennedy points out, the hierarchical model was collapsing everywhere; monarchies were disappearing in Europe and elsewhere. At the same time, in the United States the immigrant church, primarily because of education, was being assimilated into the establishment structure of American commercial and political life. For Kennedy the psychologist, the obsessive-compulsive energy of ecclesiastical authoritarianism was eventually spent. Vatican II celebrated the death of an institutional church structured largely on the authority-obedience model, and the birth of a new experience of church, at once more cooperative and collegial:

> The great symptom and sign of the collapse of the excessively dutiful psychology was the evaporation of guilt in the

---

[9]   Garden City, New York: Image Books, 1985.

[10]   *Ibid.,* p. 54.

ordinary experience of millions of Catholics. They could no longer be rewarded or punished in terms of insinuated or rumored guilt. Vatican II validated an intuition that had been growing close to consciousness in the Catholic community for many years. Lacking the authoritarian capacity to dictate the parameters of guilt, the immigrant Church witnessed a loosening in all the structures that flowed from its obsessive-compulsive ethic of authority and obedience.[11]

It was the evaporation of guilt, as Kennedy phrases it, that signaled the coming of age of American Catholicism. The child (laity) had become an adult and insisted on relating to its parent (clergy) in an adult manner.

By looking in a particular way at the use and abuse of authority within the church, Jack Costello, SJ sheds further light on the crisis of authority. He does so by borrowing the child-parent-adult psychological model developed by Eric Berne, the founder of Transactional Analysis.[12] Berne's thesis is that adult individuals or institutions tend to relate to one another in three major ways: as a child, as a parent or as an adult. To behave as an adult towards others is to recognize their equality and freedom; to behave as a parent towards others is to claim for oneself authority and responsibility; and to behave as a child is to bring out the "parent" qualities of the other. Costello applies this child-parent-adult paradigm to the relationship between laity and clergy:

> When the traditional forms of relating between clergy and laity in the church are examined through Berne's filters, we find a high proportion of them follow parent/child

---

[11]   *Ibid.,* p. 57.
[12]   See Jack Costello, SJ, "Towards An Adult Church," *Compass* (January/February, 1990), pp. 37-39.

dynamics. The church's social structures over the centuries can appear to have been deliberately cultivated on this parent/child model. Actually, this model, once all pervasive in the church, has diminished considerably since Vatican II challenged it. But in a relatively traditional Catholic culture, such as still exists for the most part in Newfoundland and other areas of the country, many people have viewed the church and clergy as representatives of truth, power and unquestionable authority.[13]

This psychological parent/child quality of the clergy-laity relationship, as developed by both Kennedy and Costello, resonates clearly with the top-down, power theology construct of the church critiqued by Rémi Parent and Leonardo Boff. In terms of ideology, and referring to the documents of Vatican II and many initiatives and exhortations since then, one could say that this model of relationship has been terminated. In practice, however, there are more than a few living remnants of parent-child relating at all levels of ecclesiastical life. It is a bitter aftertaste that does not seem to want to go away. It is precisely this "parent" attitude and behaviour on the part of some church leaders and decision-makers that continues to frustrate and disappoint many lay people.

The Crisis of Modernity

For Langdon Gilkey, the crisis in Catholicism was really brought on with its confrontation with modernity.[14] Gilkey believes that historical change is the one constant and fundamental characteristic of modernity. In taking historical change seriously, the Catholic church is finally forced to go about creatively reevaluating, reinterpreting and reformulating its life,

---

[13]   *Ibid.,* p. 38.
[14]   Langdon Gilkey, *Catholicism Confronts Modernity* (New York: The Seabury Press—A Crossroad Book, 1975).

mission and doctrine. Thus Catholicism has only recently come to acknowledge the fact that "the sacrality" of the church depends not on changelessness but on the church's faithfulness, through changing times and forms, to its mission in the world.[15] Regarding modernity, Gilkey portrays Protestantism as an elder brother to Catholicism. Protestantism has been coping with modernity for more than two hundred years. Gilkey observes that Catholicism, on the other hand, had to come to grips with that era from the Enlightenment to the 1960s in the experience called the Second Vatican Council (1961-1965). The Roman Catholic church had to deal with the social, spiritual and technological forces of three hundred years in a mere four years![16]

The opening up of Catholicism or, as Gilkey phrases it (borrowing from Pope John XXIII), the *aggiornamento* in the church has meant necessarily having to deal with the secular age:

> When the process of *aggiornamento* "opened the windows of the church" to the fresh breezes of modernity, those open windows also let in the chill blasts of naturalistic atheism and indifference, of a form of secularistic thought and life antithetical to religion of any sort and so to any interpretation of the Christian faith, ancient or modern.[17]

The secular blasts that blew in that open window along with the winds of renewal, in Gilkey's wonderfully descriptive image, offer the option of a "religionless life"—a viable, personal life without need to refer to God, church or religion: "The possibility for a secular existence appeared for the first time to countless Catholics—for whom previously a secularistic self-understanding had been literally inconceivable—the moment *aggiornamento* began."[18] Quite unintentionally, then, according to

---

15   *Ibid.,* p. 8.
16   *Ibid.,* p. 35.
17   *Ibid.,* p. 40.

Gilkey, updating has brought the church full force into the secular style of life and modernity.

What does this secular style of life look like in practice? One superficial but nonetheless telling example of secularization came to me recently while sitting in on a Grade Nine religious studies class. The class was on Sunday Eucharist and the teacher had just ascertained that less than a quarter of the students (6 of 27) and their families participate in Sunday Eucharist regularly. He then proceeded to find out why more students and their families did not attend Sunday Mass given that it was the Catholic thing to do—and they acknowledged that! The responses of the students express for me in very simple, concrete everyday language what Langdon Gilkey means by the impact of modernity on Catholicism: "Both my parents are working now, and they need to rest on Sunday"; "There are too many other things to do"; "There is always shopping that has to be done." Gilkey hints that the real problem for present-day Catholicism might very well be whether any religious existence is viable or understandable at all in modern life.

The Crisis of Understanding

Langdon Gilkey suggests that modernity presents the secular option, the religionless world that now tempts Roman Catholics. Gilkey's modernity has a definite "this world only" quality to it. The profane is front and centre; the sacred has been relegated to the periphery. David Tracy also investigates modernity, but in a philosophical manner, more from the aspect of understanding. Tracy contends that there is a modern consciousness and a postmodern consciousness.[19] A modern consciousness is above all rational, and it is supported by an unconscious

---

[18]   *Ibid.,* p. 41.

[19]   David Tracy, *Plurality And Ambiguity* (San Francisco: Harper & Row, 1987), p. 73.

optimism about the unlimited possibility of human potential. It is intellectually grounded in Socratic philosophy, the seventeenth-century scientific revolution, and the eighteenth-century Enlightenment. Politically and socially, it is expressed in the optimism of the French Revolution. It is thoroughly Western. While the traditional Christian world-view perceived reality through a supernatural lens, with singular moral and religious absolutes and absolute certainty regarding truth, the modern rationalist tends to absolutize human rationality and human potentiality. Tracy insists that a rational consciousness is clearly evident in the writing and thinking about Western history, cultural analysis, literature, philosophy and modern psychology.[20]

But Tracy argues that we are now in a postmodern era, and, therefore, a postmodern consciousness is in order. This means that all experience must now be interpreted from a new angle.

> Any postmodern position intensifies the central insight that has guided us throughout these reflections: all experience and all understanding is hermeneutical. To interpret well must now mean that we attend to and use the hermeneutics of both retrieval and suspicion.[21]

In analyzing language, David Tracy demonstrates the radical "plurality" of all language, a plurality that necessarily leads to interpretation:

> In discourse, "someone says something about something to someone . . . ." Across the whole spectrum of someone's somethings, and about somethings, we find words, sentences, paragraphs, texts. We find discourse.

---

20   *Ibid.*, p. 74.
21   *Ibid.*, p. 77.

> To discover discourse is to explore language as a reality beyond individual words in the dictionary . . . ; it is to rediscover society and history. Every discourse expresses conscious and unconscious ideologies, whether the someone who speaks or writes is aware of them or not.[22]

Thus reality and knowledge are now linked to language, and to study language is to discover the plurality of experience and understanding.

Tracy also analyzes history and discovers within it radical *ambiguity*.[23] There is not one history; there are particular histories. Postmodern reflection exposes the ideology and rediscovers the neglected or forgotten *other* in the way the dominant power recounts its own story. In other words, a particular hermeneutical stance is necessary to lay bare the ambiguous nature of history.

> To claim the ancient Israelites as our predecessors is an honor. But that claim also forces us to face the patriarchal nature of their society. We cannot forget what the Israelites did to the Canaanites and what their prayers against the children of their enemies might mean. To cherish the Christian scriptures as a charter document of liberation is entirely right. Yet we must also face its anti-Judaic strands, strands that reach us with the full history of the effects of centuries of Christian "teaching of contempt" for the Jews. And we have just begun to face the centuries of subjugation of women in Christian history—indeed, in all Western history.[24]

Plurality and *ambiguity*, according to David Tracy, best describe the nature of experience and reality.

---

22   *Ibid.,* p.61.
23   *Ibid.,* p. 70.
24   *Ibid.,* pp. 68-69.

But where is the crisis dimension in all of this, and what is the connection with Catholic culture? How, indeed, does Tracy's notion of plurality and ambiguity even remotely touch on the evangelizing activity in a Catholic school? I believe that plurality and ambiguity most adequately describe our contemporary context in all of its moral and social, intellectual and political dimensions. Will Canada exist next year, politically speaking, as it does this year? Economically speaking, will this year's high school graduates surpass their parents' standard of living in the future? In the 1970s, the answers to these questions would have been obvious. They are no longer so. Being aware of the plurality and ambiguity inherent in our ecclesial context today might also temper the ways we work for shared vision and common purpose. Certainly, if one grants the plurality and ambiguity of experience, one must then look at authority and the exercise of power in ways less hierarchical and less authoritarian. Such an admission should lead to a more dialogical, collegial sharing of responsibility. In our given ecclesial context, local churches and theologies and pastoral initiatives are more readily embraced and accepted if one is sensitive to the plurality of experience and reality. But most of all, recognizing and feeling comfortable with the plurality and ambiguity of our context today underscores the enormous urgency for the evangelizer to become interpreter! In the context of today, one does not learn by amassing data so much as by interpreting. There is an attitude, a spirit one must adopt in order to interpret. There are interpretation skills—hermeneutics of critique, suspicion and retrieval—that equip the evangelizer to see through and critique the taken-for-grantedness of assumptions and ideologies in discourse, institutional strategies and institutional life, and to retrieve the voice and experience of the neglected and forgotten other.

A Response to the Crisis

In these last few pages, I have been in dialogue with our culture, with some of the fundamental reasons why our Catholic culture is in crisis. I have come to appreciate that this crisis is far more profound than simply falling attendance at Mass, increased practice of artificial birth control, an aging clergy and a decreasing number of vocations, and the unfortunate longevity of some anachronistic customs of clerical control that simply refuse to die. These are but symptoms, I believe, of the more fundamental nature of the crisis. There is today a different way of understanding reality. David Tracy's observations about "plurality and ambiguity" become an important instrument in deciphering some of the complexity and contradictions inherent in contemporary Catholic culture. Perhaps awareness of the plurality and ambiguity of all experience was an intuition I already enjoyed before encountering Tracy. (I am not certain!) But encountering David Tracy has allowed me to describe the world in a new way, and when I can describe it in this way, I feel at once more confident and more equipped to deal with it.

Langdon Gilkey's thoughtful analysis of the Catholic crisis was also a moment of insight for me. If one opens the window for the Spirit of creative renewal, it is clear now that the chilling air of the secular age blows in as well. Gilkey describes accurately how Catholicism is actually in the midst of an enormous transition. Any transition is always risky, evoking sentiments of both fear and boldness—a fear of the future that makes one yearn for the secure past, and a boldness vis-à-vis the future in the form of a readiness to exploit the creative possibilities the moment of transition itself offers. From my dialogue with the crisis elements of Catholic culture, I believe two such creative possibilities come to the surface, possibilities that could allow us to make more sense out of the chaos and confusion of our present crisis. I believe, too, that these two possibilities are privileged means for evangelizing today.

Recovering the Catholic Idea of Sacrament

In dissecting problems and analyzing crises, one cannot help but give in to the temptation at least to hint at solutions or possible paths out of the crisis. In their reflections on the crisis of Catholic culture, Eugene Kennedy, Langdon Gilkey and Andrew Greeley go further than that. There is, in fact, a remarkable convergence in their view that the rediscovery of the Catholic principle of sacramentality might give new vitality and direction to the Catholic Christian community in crisis.

Eugene Kennedy speaks of the pastoral, sacramental sense of the Catholic church, a sacramental church that has always celebrated the critical life moments of love, suffering, death, beginning, ending, separation and reunion.[25] Revitalizing this central dimension of Catholic experience is imperative in order to move relevantly and creatively into the next century:

> The Catholic Church has kept in touch through twenty centuries with the sacramental impulses of its own mysterious heart and has retained the capacity to speak lavishly of them in symbols that transcend the law, confound excessive rationality, but reach the human heart. That capacity, long restrained, is vital for its pilgrimage into the next century.[26]

From his Protestant perspective, Langdon Gilkey acknowledges that one of the central marks of Catholicism is its "sacramentality"—the sacramental sense of the ongoing presence and activity of God in human affairs, through ordinary material, verbal and intellectual symbols. What is more, Gilkey asserts the priority of the Catholic principle of sacramental presence over

---

[25]   Kennedy, *op. cit.*, p. 146.
[26]   *Ibid.*, pp. 145-46.

the Protestant principle of the Word in our very difficult and complex modern culture.[27] Gilkey's description of modern culture resonates with David Tracy's plurality and ambiguity: all that is historical is relative! Thus, speech and discourse, words and propositions, dogmas and laws are all historically conditioned and therefore subject to qualification. Consequently, a mediation of the absolute through the word is fraught with difficulty: with plurality and ambiguity. Gilkey suggests that we are now beyond rationalism; sacramental media allow us "to recognize the finite and relative character of the media and not lose the mediation; 'symbol' is a better word than either 'dogma' or 'doctrine' on this point."[28] Gilkey notes the creative possibilities for a Catholicism that is ready to renew its profound sacramental character:

> A Catholicism that has relinquished its absolutism and has recognized the new world of relativity, and yet that as Catholic and sacramental can still relate grace and the wondrous width of divine activity to the total life-world of men and women, *this* Catholicism may well find itself more relevant to modern needs, more creative in the modern situation, and less anachronistic to modern sensibilities than any form of Protestantism.[29]

David Tracy's concept of the analogical imagination furnishes Andrew Greeley with the grounding insight for his study on how Catholics behave and believe, and why they stay in the church.[30] Greeley argues that Catholics stay in the church because they like it and because of "sacramentality"—an imagination that views creatures as metaphors for God, as hints of what God is like. This rootedness in sacramentality is what I like

---

27 Gilkey, *op. cit.*, p. 193.
28 *Ibid.*, p. 196.
29 *Ibid.*, p. 196.

to refer to as "the Catholic reflex." This imagination operates quite independently of both the institutional church and its dogmatic propositions. Using the analogical imagination as his ground, Greeley elaborates a testing instrument to determine how operative the analogical imagination continues to be in contemporary American Catholic culture. He finds it to be very much alive indeed! In Greeley's surveys, Catholics generally tended to view the values and issues he proposed in more "sacramental" ways than did Protestants. For example, Catholics value social relationships more and are more tolerant of sin and weakness; Catholics place a higher value on community than on individuality; while Protestants promote virtues of industry and initiative in their children, Catholics tend to foster loyalty, obedience and patience; Protestants are more likely to deplore anything that detracts from the individual's integrity and freedom, while Catholics take exception to actions that take away from community; and while Catholics emphasize the social and institutional aspects of religion, Protestants underscore personal devotion and responsibility. In a word, Catholics tend to see a God who reveals himself sacramentally—through ordinary human symbols and instruments, while Protestants,

---

[30]   Greeley, *op. cit.*, Chapter 3, "Do Catholics Imagine Differently?" My discussion is based largely on Greely's development of the Catholic imagination here.

According to David Tracy, an analogical imagination views God as present in the world and revealing himself in and through creation. Thus, the world and its artifacts are somewhat like God. They are symbols mediating God's presence. This is a sacramental imagination and from Tracy's study of the Catholic classics, this imagination tends to characterize Catholics.

Protestants, on the other hand, imagine differently. The Protestant imagination is dialectical: God is radically absent from the world and reveals himself only rarely—the Christ event! So the world and all of its artifacts are vastly different from God. Tracy's study of the Protestant classics yields a Protestant imagination: the individual tends to stand apart from society, suspicious of it. Thus there is an accent on individualism rather than community.

because of their individualist ethic, see a God out there, opposite and radically different from the world.

In a subsequent study, Greeley confirms the attraction and hold that "sacramentality" has on the Catholic imagination. From a list of thirteen reasons for being and remaining Catholic,[31] Greeley finds that sacraments and a faith to pass on to children are the most important reasons for remaining Catholic and for not leaving the church; and the hold sacramentality has on Catholics tends to temper the anger and diminish the effect of dissatisfaction with the institution because of realities such as clericalism and the lack of respect for women.[32]

Thus, from his work with David Tracy's notion of the analogical imagination, Andrew Greeley reaches the following conclusion regarding sacramentality:

> Catholics stay in the Church because they like being Catholic, because of loyalty to the imagery of the Catholic imagination, because of pictures of a loving God present in creation, because of the spiritual vision of Catholics that they absorbed in their childhood, along with and often despite all the rules and regulations that were drummed into their heads. They leave, or think of leaving, because of the failure of church leadership to live up to that spiritual vision.[33]

---

[31]   See Andrew M. Greeley's essay "Sacraments Keep Catholics High on the Church," *National Catholic Reporter* (April 12, 1991), pp. 12-13. Greeley proposes the following reasons for remaining Catholic: an explanation of life; rules on how to love; religious certainty; rich heritage of the past; a faith to pass on to children; consolation in times of sorrow; support of a community; something to bind the family and marriage together; the sacraments; parish life and activities; strong religious authority; help from parish; infallible papal teaching.

[32]   *Ibid.,* p. 13.

[33]   Greeley, *The Catholic Myth,* p. 63.

Sacramentality runs deep in the Catholic psyche and defines the Catholic imagination. It seems that at this moment in the Catholic crisis, it is an aspect of Catholic heritage that is under-valued and tended to largely in routine, unimaginative ways. Sacramentality needs to be creatively reclaimed. Langdon Gilkey values sacramentality and emphasizes both its theological centrality and the priority it should have in evangelization in a modern culture with a postmodern consciousness. And Andrew Greeley demonstrates empirically the priority "the sacraments" *de facto* enjoy in the behaviour and beliefs of Catholic lay people. I believe that there is a critical question raised here concerning the way we now go about Catholic education: could it be that we are privileging the Protestant principle of the Word (which would seem to be the logical option, given that the whole enterprise of education has been "word" or *logos* based!) to the neglect of the Catholic principle of the sacrament? My own hunch is that we are. There is neither time nor space to pursue this question further, but it is a question that deserves attention.[34]

Interpretation: A Dimension of Evangelization

Langdon Gilkey writes of the implications of the relativity of history. According to David Tracy, all reality is marked by

---

[34] Several questions present themselves here, all of great importance for Catholic education. The way we do religious education now is for the most part classroom-centred and word-centred. A privileging of sacramentality would favour experience: prayer, mystery, the retreat experience. Also, a sacramental imagination presupposes socialization into the sacraments. But how effectively can schools socialize into the sacraments without a reasonable commitment on the part of parents or parent? And that in turn raises the thorny parish/school/home partnership question. The new ecclesial reality locates the school as the place for primary socialization into the church: how can sacramental initiation be integrated even more completely into the Catholic school community, and what will this mean for many pastors who see the parish as the focal point of the life and faith of the church?

plurality and ambiguity, and so all experience must be interpreted. A hermeneutical stance is necessary. But Tracy notes as well that even through hermeneutics, the best one can arrive at is only a relatively adequate claim for certainty: "Theologians cannot escape the same plurality and ambiguity that affect all discourse."[35]

In *Plurality And Ambiguity,* David Tracy speaks of "interpretation" in several ways: critique, openness to the plurality of language and the ambiguity of history, suspicion, and retrieval.[36] For Tracy, there are two distinct aspects of interpretation: resistance and hope.

[M]y principal concern in this narrative has been to describe a more modest but crucial hope, and one suggested by the conflict of interpretations on interpretation itself. That hope is this: that all those involved in interpreting our situation and all those aware of our need for solidarity may continue to risk interpreting all the classics of all the traditions. And in that effort to interpret lie both resistance and hope.[37]

Resistance is resistance to the *status quo,* the given of our present life situation, the powers and ideologies of our time and place. *Hope* is both steadfast confidence in God's continued presence and action in our present life-situation and struggle,

---

[35] Tracy, *op. cit.,* p. 84. See also p. 99, where Tracy elaborates the theme of the tentativeness of interpreting the religious classics. He notes that in interpretation everything is at risk: there is ambiguity in the interpreter's own understanding; there is the plurality inherent in the text; there is the ambiguity of the time and place out of which the text was fashioned; there is the ambiguity inherent in the conversation, the method whereby the interpreter works at interpreting the text. At best, one can only achieve a relatively adequate understanding; and this relatively adequate understanding, in turn, will become relatively inadequate when new questions and insights emerge.

[36] *Ibid.,* Chapter 5, "Resistance and Hope: The Question of Religion."

[37] *Ibid.,* p. 114.

and the hope for the authenticity and goodness that could be. I see this spirit of resistance and hope as foundational in doing ministry today. Consequently, because of the pluralistic and ambiguous reality in which we live and in which the church evangelizes, interpretation in ministry is imperative. Indeed, it is unavoidable. It is perhaps the one absolute in our constantly changing context. Tracy hints at the source of the plurality and ambiguity that so mark our contemporary context for ministry in the fundamental religious or limit questions he poses—"questions attendant upon an acknowledgement of the historical and social contingency of all the values embraced and all the convictions lived by."[38] In speaking of "values embraced and convictions lived by," my feeling is that we are not speaking here only of abstract, philosophical theology. Rather, this also means the stuff of everyday life, which in turn, is the stuff of ministry. And it is this *stuff* that demands interpretation in ministry, especially the ministry of Catholic education.

Plurality and ambiguity are part and parcel of our contemporary ecclesial context. To the Catholic educator familiar with the worlds of both teacher and student, the context of plurality and ambiguity presents an awesome challenge to evangelization. Many teachers today admit that they are confused and insecure. They have questions: how to read the signs of the times; how to select what is appropriate and adequate; how to make sense of or deal with the mixed signals emanating from our social and ecclesial context. Some teachers have been raised religiously on absolutes and certainty. Historical and social contingency regarding faith values and church teaching are unthinkable. Thus they are not at all at ease in the context of plurality and ambiguity. Some teachers, on the other hand, are seriously questioning and are

---

[38]   *Ibid.*, p. 86.

engaged in strategies of resistance and hope in David Tracy's sense of interpretation.[39]

Interpretation can also be understood as a dimension of evangelization. As I remarked above, to be able to name the plurality and ambiguity so operative in our experience is already a step in coping. Interpretation, when understood as an aspect of evangelization, can mean a more dialogical, cooperative, collegial approach to the ministry of Catholic education. Plurality must be respected. A desire to arrive at even the most relatively adequate certainty means conversation rather than argument.[40] I

---

[39] I offer the following two testimonies to concretize the problems that plurality and ambiguity pose for Catholic teachers. At the same time, the questions raised in these examples underscore the need that teachers have to cultivate the spirit of interpretation and hone the skills for interpreting. These two testimonies are from personal conversations during staff faith development sessions:

February, 1991—An English Teacher

Most of the time I am confident when religious and moral questions arise in class discussion that I am faithful to church tradition and teachings. But on occasion I have reached the point where I am not sure: how much of what I offer is me, or mine? How much of it is what the church teaches? This bothers me. How do I know?

February, 1991—A Religion Teacher

I have to meet with the young priest in our parish. He is in his early 30s. He has this thing about respect for authority. He gets after me for saying "Bishop" instead of "Your Excellency". Often in his preaching he'll come back to the authority question. He links truth with authority: "If we don't respect authority, we'll never get the truth!" I find it sad. This young man is living in another world! He said on Sunday: "George Bush is authority, so George Bush must have the truth regarding the Gulf War." We are educated people in the parish. How can he expect us to accept that stuff? And how do I untangle this confusion for my students?

[40] In *Plurality And Ambiguity,* Chapter 1, "Interpretation, Conversation, Argument," David Tracy develops his idea of conversation and prescribes rules that should govern any conversation used to interpret. It is by following a question in conversation—with a person, a text, a situation—that one goes about interpreting.

see such cooperation and such conversation as being of the gospel. It follows for Catholic education, then, that interpretation takes place in the context of community; the solidarity of voices who support and critique is in order!

There is, too, a *witness* quality inherent in the notion of interpretation as a dimension of evangelization. Students working through the adolescent socialization stage of identity need access to the spirit and skills of interpretation. In this instance the teacher can evangelize by modelling interpretation for students through one's own engagement in life and in life's questions. Such an engagement would be an engagement of resistance and an engagement of hope. In a more practical way, skills for interpretation can be developed concretely through courses that emphasize media literacy and the critique implied in social analysis.

I believe that it is very helpful for the teacher in the Catholic high school to look at herself/himself as an interpreter. Furthermore, I am convinced that interpretation as I have described it can be an effective element in evangelizing in the Catholic high school. For the teacher and for the teachers who make up the core of the Christian community within the school, this means that as evangelizers they must themselves be evangelized; and as interpreters, they themselves must adopt the spirit of interpretation and work at adopting skills for interpretation. There are ways to go about interpreting; there are strategies that can help make interpretation more pertinent.[41] For me, the plurality and ambiguity of our present context have put in relief the act of resistance and hope, the urgency of interpreting, of being able to arrive at a course of action, a response to a question, a piece of truth that seems relevant and adequate for here and now. Teachers in the Catholic school need to appreciate the plurality and ambiguity of much of our religious context; they need the confidence to choose and decide for themselves, to own their own faith; they need the understanding that in so interpreting, they model this adult faith for the students in their care.

---

41   From a reflection on my own experience as a Catholic educator and in dialogue with other Catholic educators, these are some principles for interpretation in Catholic education that I have found to be helpful:

1. A knowledge and love of Jesus and the gospels. In the beginning of John's Gospel, the disciples ask Jesus: "Where do you live?" Jesus invites them: "Come and see!"

2. A love for the church—for the Vatican II expression of the mission of the church.

3. A critical spirit—self, church, society, and Catholic education efforts.

4. An ongoing cultural and social analysis and the openness and readiness to receive from the world.

5. The preferential option for the poor.

6. The solidarity of community.

7. Openness to suffering and set-backs.

8. The human qualities of graciousness, tolerance and respect.

IV

A Reflection on the Ministry of a Priest-Educator

In Chapter 1, I traced some of the critical theological moments, both academic and pastoral, that have impressed and informed me and have helped fashion my present ministry as priest-teacher and Catholic educator, as well as my present preoccupations in ministry. In Chapter 2, I proposed some fundamental ecclesiological ideals and commented on the model of church I embrace and that, ideally at least, I hope would govern my endeavours in and attitude towards ministry. I also gave colour and contour to evangelization as a theology of mission, a theology that I feel most appropriately describes what Catholic education could be and should be. In this chapter, I would like to digress for a moment and reflect on images of ministry that are important to me and reveal some of my preoccupations and approaches as I continue to live and work with a special focus on Catholic education in the ordained ministry of the Roman Catholic Christian community. In doing so, I hope to synthesize some of the central ideas I have touched on so far.

Images of Ministry

From Scripture

My image of ministry is tied up with my image of church. I appreciate the Vatican II image "pilgrim church." I like the dynamic quality of pilgrimage. I am taken with the historical connectedness of the pilgrimage image. Perhaps the Hebrew Scriptures' exodus and forty-year pilgrimage experience with its uncertainty and ambiguity mean more to me than a Lourdes-type pilgrimage where the goal—the point of arrival—is unmistakable.

Rémi Parent proposes "the nomad" as a symbol for the church, and this symbol, I believe captures the same dynamic, historical and faith-rooted meaning of the pilgrim church:

> It is its nature to be on the march, and nomadism is part of its definition. In short, the Church only exists when it is passing from a standardizing clericalism to communion, and, in spite of our dreams that it will be otherwise, it will always exist this way if it really wishes to be the sacrament of the passover of Jesus.[1]

The images of *nomad* and *pilgrim* evoke a movement—a people always in passage in history. And because of the journey or movement of this people, church is never attained, but is always being made, always becoming.

Minister as pilgrim, minister as nomad—these images are meaningful to me. The nomad has the daily task of charting the journey, of interpreting the way. The pilgrim must be faithful to the Word and the Promise. The pilgrim's fidelity can be assured only by listening and interpreting and reinterpreting the Word on the way.

---

[1]   Parent, *op. cit.,* p. 142.

Fidelity to the Word provides nourishment. A sustaining Word for me in ministry is John 15: 1-17—Jesus the true vine. This Word roots me in discipleship. Before the apostles were a community, they were the disciples of Jesus. And once becoming a community of apostles, their first priority was to be true to discipleship—to the life and message of Jesus, the Lord.[2] Another Word that challenges me in ministry today is the prophetic Word. I interpret this Word, I understand it, as Jesus' Word and intention for the church today. I take Luke 4: 16-22 at face value: Jesus came to bring Good News to the poor. I understand this to be Jesus' intention, as well, for his community of disciples. And the Word of judgement in Matthew 25: 31-46 is more than simply the individualistic, private caution that the community over the centuries has attached to it. I prefer the historical interpretation, pregnant with social, political and economic analysis and challenges, that liberation theology understands in this Word. This was the bold and prophetic exegesis given by Pope John Paul II in Edmonton in September, 1984.

From Our Contemporary Context

But there are images for ministry, too, that arise from the context in which one ministers and, as I have already illustrated, a context of crisis—the climate of plurality and ambiguity that now conditions church life and practice—makes for a more complex and oftentimes more difficult context in which to minister. Gregory Baum names our contemporary socio-political and ecclesiastical context "the wilderness":

---

2   Edward Schillebeeckx insists on the primacy of discipleship in the constitution of the apostolic and post-apostolic Christian communities. See: Edward Schillebeeckx, *Ministry: Leadership in the Community of Jesus Christ* (New York: Crossroad, 1982), p. 36.

In my judgement, this "kairos" (the special time beginning
with the 1960s when major social change toward greater
justice was an historical possibility) is over. We now live in
"the wilderness." The new politico-economic situation and
the corresponding cultural trends have, moreover, affected
the life and the policies of the Christian churches. Retrench-
ment is the order of the day. Will the World Council of
Churches survive the present trend where each church
concentrates on its own confessional identity? In the Catholic church the new emphasis on identity is making the hierarchy more self-involved, putting brakes on its involvement
with other churches, its association with other religions, and
its cooperation with secular movements. Fear is becoming
the church's counselor.[3]

The wilderness, however, is not foreign land for the nomad or
the pilgrim. Time and experience there can be discouraging, but
it can also be time for preparation, for the deepening of one's
resolve to continue to struggle for the Kingdom.

For Karl Rahner, speaking in the early 1980s, our present
context is more like winter.[4] Rahner saw the Western church, in

---

[3]   Gregory Baum, "Good-bye to the Ecumenist," *The Ecumenist* (Vol. 29,
No. 2/Spring, 1991), p.2.

[4]   See Karl Rahner, SJ, *Faith In A Wintry Season: Conversations and In-
terviews with Karl Rahner in the Last Years of His Life* (New York: Crossroads,
1990). See p. 75 and "A Wintry Church and the Opportunities for Christianity,"
pp. 184-200. In elaborating his notion of wintry church, Rahner holds up Vatican
II and its spirit as the point of reference and comparison. Vatican II opened up
new possibilities, but "present Roman centralism" puts a damper on that spirit
and restricts the possibilities. He argues that more decentralization is needed: in
liturgy, in Canon Law, in the possibility for the world-church to be realized in the
evolution of local churches, and in inculturation. Perhaps Rahner's greatest disappointment is that the demands of the future church are so clear and the possibilities for creative pastoral planning so great, yet nothing seems to be happening
because of unimaginative Roman officialdom and mediocre hierarchical leadership.

particular, to be in "the wintry season." The euphoria of Vatican II was probably responsible for too many high expectations; the fragile and very human institution and structures could not meet those expectations. So the church, like the earth and human life itself, Rahner contends, has its seasons, and "winter" seems most apt to describe our present church season. Winter is gray and dreary; winter signals a certain temporary death for plant life and vegetation; winter can be cold and stormy. As a minister today, in the Roman Catholic Christian community, my ministry takes place in a climate that seems to be more wintry than spring-like!

Ministering in the Wintry Season

Part of the wintry context, of course, is due to my own frailty, inadequacy and infidelity as a minister. But there is, as well, the "sin of our fathers" (probably a more accurate phrasing than the inclusive "ancestors" in this case) that has been so influential in shaping the church's present wintry season. Ours is a tradition profoundly conditioned by patriarchal clericalism, especially in the practice of ministry. Ministry in this context can be personally distressing. I am a cleric-preacher not at all comfortable with the clerical structure of the church. The clerical structure, as we have seen, dis-empowers and alienates. It is an obstacle to mutuality and communion. It has tended to promote and maintain mediocrity in proclamation, celebration and administration. I am in and of that structure. My theology of preaching is critically important for me in my role as priest. The homily is proclamation. I believe strongly in the Barthian theology of the Word: the Lord is active in the act of proclamation. I do not believe that the Lord works *ex opere operato* in the proclamation, and Sunday is an anxious time for me. I cannot escape the fact that, as cleric, I am front and centre. I know in my heart and head and gut that more than a few of my sisters are hurting because of what I represent. Yet I still feel the call to proclaim. This is for me a costly consequence of the ambiguity that colours the whole of church life and work today. *Resistance*, here, happens necessarily in the form of an ongoing interpretation constantly trying to integrate and to make sense of it all: vocation to preach, patriarchal clerical church, the imperative to stand with those oppressed by the structures, a relevant critical theology of preaching, and so on. *Hope* lies in the trust that oppressive structures can be transformed.

There is, too, the incredibility/credibility tension of the church that I encounter as minister. As both priest-preacher and priest-teacher, I know well the incredibility of the clerical, patriarchal church. At the same time I know intimately (because it has so nourished my own life and meaning) the truth and goodness and graciousness (graced-ness) of the church. I know what makes the church credible. As a minister I find myself in a permanent state of ambiguity, conflict and tension between that which makes the church credible and that which makes the church incredible. There is more than a little cost involved for the nomad who pitches tent in that in-between wintry space. I see much of my ministry, as I have already suggested, in terms of interpretation: interpreting boldly that which makes the church credible, and interpreting even more boldly (in the sense of critique) that which makes the church incredible.

But even in the midst of winter there are occasional days with warm sun and bright blue skies that hint of spring. And so it is in ministering in the wintry season. There is a profoundly rich dimension of blessing to the teaching tradition of the Roman Catholic community that continues to develop and is nurturing in its development. I refer again to some of the texts that helped form me: *The Church in the Modern World* (1965), *On the Development of Peoples* (1967), *On Evangelization* (1975), The Canadian Bishops' "Ethical Reflections on the Economic Crisis" (1982), *Concern for the Social Order* (1987) and the recent Bishops' Statement, "Widespread Unemployment—A Call to

Mobilize the Social Forces of the Nation" (1993). Within these documents there is a theology of empowerment waiting to be liberated and implemented. These are seeds of great hope; this is evidence that there is a creative and prophetic voice in the leadership of the church.

The Roman Catholic community is a structured community. In much of this chapter I have been critical of distortions in the structures, especially of clericalism. I appreciate John Coleman's development of the theology of ordained ministry.[5] Coleman sees three essential characteristics of ordained ministry:

- the ordo or order of ordained ministry, which makes provision for permanency, stability and public character necessary for ministry in the church;

- the sacramental nature of ordained ministry, in which the ordained minister focuses on the sacramental life of the church and is a representative type of the church;

- the collegial nature of ordained ministry, by which bishops, priests and deacons represent the church not as individuals but as a collectivity.[6]

I am enriched and renewed by this theology. It is a piece of relatively adequate meaning for me in the wintry season.

There is a new collaboration at large today in the Roman Catholic communion. The old dichotomies—male/female, clergy/laity—are breaking down. We are recovering the community dimension to all ministry: basic Christian communities, pastoral teams, life communities. Increasingly, the lived experi-

---

5   See John A. Coleman, SJ, "A Theology of Ministry," *The Way* (Vol. 25, January, 1985) pp. 7-18.

6   *Ibid.*, pp. 13-14.

ence of the followers of Jesus is becoming the privileged place and source for the interpretation of God's Word today.

In my own personal pilgrimage as a minister in the Canadian Roman Catholic community, I am always being challenged and renewed by the sisters and brothers in local churches across the world. It is the *globalité* or "internationality" of the church, and the necessary pluralism implied, that inspires creativity and many new understandings and initiatives that can be shared and adapted in communal mutuality. Fortunately, the English Canadian church has the Quebec church; the North American church has the Latin American church; these are not situations of dependency, but of mutual sharing.

Finally, within the ministry of Catholic education, I continue to be encouraged and challenged by some Catholic educators, not great in numbers, but radical in their commitment to be transforming salt and leaven in their communities, and to model that commitment to the students in their care and the colleagues working at their side. This, more than anything else, gives me hope for Catholic education.

There are more than a few hints of spring in this wintry season of the church!

V

The Meaning of Formation for Catholic Education

The theological and cultural foundations I have developed in Chapters 2 and 3 are necessary to understand my vision of Catholic education. They are important and useful in appreciating some of the critical questions emerging around the doing of Catholic education today. Consequently, I feel that these theoretical foundations are of considerable value for a reflection on the formation question in Catholic education: how to prepare teachers to teach in a *Catholic* school.

There are other foundations that must still be explained before I go on to describe my model of formation. My understanding of formation and of formation as adult learning, my adaptation of shared praxis as a process for formation, and my notion of theological reflection on the Catholic education story—these concepts are central to the process I employ in Part Three. I consider them to be foundations, in both an educational and a methodological sense. It is now my intention to complete this section on the foundations by presenting an explanation of each and to indicate why and how each educational concept is significant in the model of formation I propose.

Formation

In Chapter 1, I concluded that there is a formation void in Catholic education and that this is a fundamental weakness. I contend that teachers are not formed adequately to be able to translate into effective action and behaviour the awesome demands, expectations and ideals that are part and parcel of the vocation of the Catholic educator. My bias, as I also explained in Chapter 1, is that to teach in a Catholic high school is a "vocation"; the teacher is called to serve in a special way (through the Catholic school and Catholic education) in furthering the mission of the church. In Chapter 2, I further described the vocation of the Catholic educator as the call to evangelize: to talk about the Good News and to witness to Jesus Christ by one's actions, life priorities and willingness to share faith. It follows, then, that a special preparation is needed to teach in a *Catholic* school and that both initial and ongoing training are needed to discern and live out the exigencies of the vocation of Catholic educators. *Formation* is the term I prefer to describe this "preparation and training."

For me, formation for Catholic teachers is invitational, not forced. It is not brain-washing or propagandizing in the sense of imposing an ideology or a set of dogmatic principles and prescriptions as to what a teacher must or must not do. Rather, formation is more holistic in that it attempts to touch the person's spirit, to awaken within the person the notion that teaching in a Catholic school is more than just a job or even a profession. It is a vocation.

Formation is a notion that is built into the post-Vatican II way of Catholic life. In religious life, for example, each community has a formation program. There is a "constitution on formation" in a community's rule of life on how to initiate a candidate into the spirit, charism and demands of the apostolate for the particular community. There are significant stages of formation: pre-novitiate, novitiate, post-novitiate, final profession. There is, too, an important new emphasis on ongoing or continuing formation for professed religious of all ages.[1] This formation is holistic: it is concerned with much more than just job training and the attainment of skills.

For the laity, too, there has been a proliferation of renewal and adult faith learning programs in the Catholic church since Vatican II. In his 1988 exhortation *On the Vocation and Mission*

---

[1]   Two paragraphs from the Constitutions of the Congregation of Holy Cross describe both initial and life-long formation.

(56) The disciples followed the Lord Jesus in his ministry of proclaiming the Kingdom and healing the afflicted. Jesus also spent long days alone with his disciples, speaking to them of the mysteries of his Kingdom and forming them to the point when they, too, could be sent on his mission. Later they would return for his comment and for a deeper hearing because of what they had experienced. Later still they were visited by the fire of his Spirit, who transformed their understanding of all he had ever taught them. We, too, are sent to his mission as men formed and in need of lifelong formation for his service.

(76) It is commonly imagined that our formation is most extensive when we are beginners. But often our most radical formative experiences come upon us when we are well into adulthood. Indeed, we can better grasp and accept profound self-scrutiny, the questioning of our established assumptions and ambitions, and deepening initiation into Christ when we have walked the path of adult experience and responsibility. Programs of continuing renewal in the community are one very helpful way of sharing that lifelong formation. Lifelong formation is lifelong growth.

Again, without wanting to indoctrinate or to turn teacher preparation into formation for religious life, there **are** formation elements in these two paragraphs that are most applicable and appropriate for a formation experience for Catholic educators:

• the notion of vocation—of being sent on a mission;
• the need to listen to Jesus and his words;
• the reflection *in community* on the experience of being on mission;
• the need to reflect on experience and the fact that adult experience itself becomes the stuff out of which ongoing formation takes place.

of the Lay Faithful (Christifideles Laici), Pope John Paul II underscores the importance of formation for the Catholic laity to live out their vocation as the followers of Jesus.[2]

For Catholic educators in particular, their training and preparation is spoken of as formation in the post-Vatican II church. "The Formation That Is Needed If Lay Catholics Are To Give Witness To The Faith In A School" is the cumbersome title given to Part Three of the 1982 Vatican document, *Lay Catholics in Schools: Witnesses to Faith.*[3] In spite of the awkward heading, the content is important:

> The concrete living out of a vocation as rich and profound as that of the lay Catholic in a school requires an appropriate formation, both on the professional plane and on the religious plane . . . . The need for an adequate formation is often felt most acutely in religious and spiritual areas: all too frequently, lay Catholics have not had a religious formation that is equal to their general, cultural, and, most especially, professional formation.[4]

There is formation needed over and above the technical and systematic training provided by faculties of education. In their

---

[2]   Pope John Paul II, *Vocation and Mission of the Lay Faithful (Christifideles Laici)* (Sherbrooke, Quebec: Éditions Paulines, 1989). In No. 59, John Paul II speaks of an integrated formation. He warns against two parallel lives: concrete daily life and existence on the one hand and spirituality and faith on the other. In this passage he is eloquent about the need to avoid dualism and rather to see faith penetrating and giving direction to all dimensions of one's life. He insists that formation and ongoing formation are essential for accomplishing this. In No. 60, John Paul outlines areas of formation that should be tended to, to yield the "unity of life" he proposes: spiritual formation, doctrinal formation, church social teaching, and the cultivation of human and cultural values.

[3]   *Lay Catholics in Schools: Witnesses to Faith* (Rome: Congregation for Catholic Education, 1982).

[4]   *Ibid.*, No. 60.

1989 pastoral letter on education, *This Moment of Promise*, the Ontario Bishops emphasize the need for continuing or ongoing faith development "if teachers hope to meet the challenge of this moment—the challenge of forming educational communities of faith."[5]

Based on this brief survey of the meaning of *formation* in the post-Vatican II church, there are several points that one should underline about the meaning and importance of *formation:*

• *Formation* is training, but it is much more than training. Formation attends to the vocation dimension of teaching in the Catholic school. The Catholic educator aware of her/his vocation is serious about growing in faith and owning one's faith. The person of Jesus and his Good News must figure prominently in any formation experience, inviting the teacher and challenging and questioning her/him. There is much to know intellectually about faith and evangelization, but there is the even greater need to respond in an affective way to Jesus who is the content of evangelization.

• *Formation* is most effective when it attends to the experience of the one being formed and the context in which the formation experience takes place. The circumstances, daily happenings, persons, problems and questions, personal approaches and reactions, successes and failures, all constitute the critical stuff of a formation experience.

• *Formation* has a certain dimension of mutuality. It happens best when peers or collaborators reflect together on their common mission. They are adult learners together, forming one another.

---

[5]   *This Moment of Promise*, p. 27.

• *Formation* for Catholic educators includes taking seriously the challenge to form an adult faith community that itself becomes the core of the formative community that is the school. One of the insights of Catholic education is the value and importance of doing education in community.

• *Formation* is ongoing. It is not a one-time experience that results in a Type A or Specialist Certificate. Formation is ongoing because the vocation of teaching in the Catholic school is not something static. It is dynamic. Formation is ongoing because the context is forever changing, and Jesus continues to invite us to respond in new and creative ways.

Formation, then, is much more than a training course or development in pedagogical methods and skills. In no way is it my intention to substitute or supplant what is now done in the faculties of education vis-à-vis teacher training. I am convinced, however, that teachers entering the separate school system need something more. If the Catholic school system is to have continued moral reasons for existence, then Catholic educators must grow in their understanding of the vocation dimension of teaching in a Catholic school. The moment a teacher begins to grasp an awareness of the vocation dimension, the formation experience also begins, and it will continue to take place as long as the teacher sincerely attends to it. Attending to the vocation is "the something more" required of the Catholic educator.

Formation as Adult Learning

The model of formation I elaborate is founded on adult learning principles.[6] Adult learning differs significantly from a

---

[6]   I am indebted to Dr. Marge Denis and her Toronto School of Theology course, "Facilitating Adult Learning in Ministry," given in April-May, 1990, for my understanding of "adult learning principles."

more classical, teacher-centered approach to learning, which, unfortunately, can still be found in high schools. In the former, the experience of all is valued. Adults have accumulated a wide range of life experiences and have developed a foundation, a core of former experiences to which they can relate new ideas and insights. This rich experience-base means that they have much to share. In the latter, on the other hand, it is the experience of the teacher that is privileged. The teacher's experience, not the learner's, becomes the primary resource in the educational dynamic, thus making it more a teaching activity than a learning experience.

In adult learning there is a certain reciprocity or interdependence that characterizes the learning experience. Adults accept responsibility for their own learning, and in doing so, they mutually benefit and enrich one another. An authentic adult learning experience is inevitably an empowering experience. But in teacher-focused pedagogy, the teacher-learner relationship is still fundamentally one of dependence: the student depends on the teacher. The teacher directs the learner. The teaching act is so structured that the teacher does not intentionally learn from the student.

The readiness of the adult learner is a third characteristic of adult learning. The particular learning experience makes sense for the adult learner. There is interest in the topic and something of value that can be applied immediately to one's life situation. In the more classical, pedagogical approach to education, readiness is very much a hit-and-miss proposition. The content is pre-designed. Classes are established to follow a structured curriculum. It is only occasionally that a topic will pique the learner's interest and have immediate relevance, and when it does happen, it is for the most part accidental.

It is clear that the formation model I propose really is adult learning. The life experience of the teacher and the experiences of the teachers and students together in the school community become the prime stuff out of which the vocation of the Catholic teacher can be nurtured and developed. It is this stuff—personal and mutual experiences—that is reflected upon and shared in a collaborative, non-threatening way. This is the type of sharing that enriches and empowers, affirms and challenges. It is this interdependent reflective experience of Catholic educators that can offer clarity and give focus to one's own understanding of what it is to be a Catholic teacher. As well, there is the communal dimension to this interdependent sharing: the core Christian community of the school (committed adult teachers) can become more aware of its common mission to become a formative community for the young people in their care. Part Three offers numerous concrete examples of this sharing-as-formation.

I have insisted that a formation experience should be invitational: the readiness factor is critical. When Catholic teachers are ready, I believe, a genuine formation experience is possible. Formation cannot be forced; it cannot be programmed or mandated. The invitation to the teachers, however, can be coloured and shaped with elements of challenge. There can be a questioning dimension to the invitation that gently encourages teachers to get serious about attending to their vocation as Catholic educators. The fundamental intuition deriving from my own experience is that the majority of teachers will reach stages of readiness for further formation: the interest in and quest for a deeper understanding of Catholic education or a new openness or willingness to be more effective evangelizers will be present at different moments in a teacher's life journey. It is at such moments that a formation experience is called for.

Formation through "Shared Praxis"

The renowned religious educator Thomas Groome has formulated a shared praxis model of religious education which consists of five movements which he grounds in the concrete experience and practice of Jesus.[7] Elements of Groome's model are valuable in the elaboration of my own model of formation for Catholic educators.

1. Jesus took the initiative to go into towns and villages and to invite people to accept his word.

    Movement One – **Looking at one's own life in faith.** The inquirer, the questioner, the seeker is invited to look at "the ultimacy questions" in her/his life.

2. Jesus would invite his hearers to look deeper into their own lives and reflect on them. Jesus invites people to look critically at their own present praxis.

    Movement Two – **Critical reflection upon one's own life in faith.** The inquirer is invited to a sharper, more detailed review of her/his life and present praxis: what are the significant biographical moments? What is the evolving social context? What are the influences on you at the core of your being? Why?

---

[7]   Thomas Groome, "Shared Praxis: An 'Ordinary' Approach to Evangelization," *Catholic Evangelization Today*, ed. Kenneth Boyak, CSP (New York/Mahwah: Paulist Press, 1987), pp. 145-159. In Groome's *Sharing Faith—A Comprehensive Approach to Religious Education and Pastoral Ministry: The Way of Shared Praxis* (San Francisco: Harper Collins, 1991), he defines *shared praxis* as

   a participative and dialogical pedagogy in which people reflect critically on their own historical agency in time and place and on their sociocultural reality, have access together to Christian story/vision, and personally appropriate it in community with the creative intent of renewed praxis in Christian faith toward God's reign for all creation (p. 135).

3. Jesus shared with his hearers the good news: "God's reign is at hand."

    Movement Three – **The Christian story and vision.** The evangelizer presents to the inquirer the essential elements of the Christian story.

4. Jesus had a great respect for the freedom of his hearers. Jesus invited people to listen to him and follow him: he did not force them to hear and follow.

    Movement Four – **Making the story one's own.** The inquirers are led gently to come to appropriate the Christian story as their own. The freedom of the inquirer must be respected. Faith is unique to each person. The inquirer cannot live the evangelizer's faith but must come to accept and own faith for oneself.

5. Jesus called people to decision, to change their lives. The faith response that Jesus evoked was more than intellectual assent. It was affective, touching the heart as well as the mind.

    Movement Five – **Inviting decision for lived Christian faith.** The evangelizer, like Jesus, will at some point invite the inquirer to a decision to accept and follow Jesus in everyday life and to embrace all of the consequences— political, social, economic—of that decision.

Groome's process is clearly based on the conversation or relationship between the inquirer and the evangelizer. He presupposes that the inquirer is not intimate with the Christian story but has sufficient interest to realize that that same story has the possibility of making meaning in her/his own life.

I find great merit in Thomas Groome's five stages of shared praxis, and I feel that his process can be adapted to structure a formative conversation among believers looking critically at their common vocation as Catholic educators. There are three elements in particular that I would borrow from Groome and adapt to create a model of formation for Catholic teachers:

1. To look at one's vocation as a Catholic educator critically (Movements 1 and 2);

2. To reflect on and retell the Christian story in light of one's own practice and experience as a Catholic educator (Movement 3);

3. To own the Christian story even more so that one's vocation in Catholic education is affirmed with new clarity, energy and purpose (Movements 4 and 5).

Groome remarks that the conversation between the inquirer and the evangelizer is not only an evangelizing experience for the former, but for the latter as well. In evangelizing, the evangelizer is evangelized too:

> We must remember that the act of evangelizing is always a "two way street." In evangelizing we also become evangelized. Getting on with the task of evangelization may well be among the most effective ways of renewing our faith community. Surely that lesson has been learned from our parishes that have attempted to implement the Rite of Christian Initiation of Adults (RCIA). The efforts to recruit and form new members in Christian living has been a powerful source of reform for the parishes themselves.[8]

In the model of formation I elaborate, this mutuality of the evangelizing act is most significant. A group of committed Catholic educators, aware of their vocation as Catholic educators, reflect on their experience and share with a group of teachers new to the Catholic school and only beginning to understand the vocation

---

[8]   Groome, "Shared Praxis: An 'Ordinary' Approach to Evangelization," p. 150.

dimension of being a Catholic educator. While it is expected that the new teachers will grow in appropriating for themselves a deeper understanding of vocation, the committed teachers will, in turn, be evangelized—by the new teachers, by other committed teachers, and by the very experience of revisiting and retelling the Christian story.

Formation through a Shared Reflection on Experience as Catholic Educators

Thomas Groome's Third Movement of the shared praxis model is "to make present the Christian story/vision." I adapt this movement to situate the telling (or, "retelling" in my model) of the Christian story in terms of one's own practice and experience in Catholic education. In fact I go even further, and suggest that Catholic educators "tell and retell the Catholic education story," since the Christian story, if our Catholic education is to be authentic, must be at the very heart of the Catholic education story. In the model of formation I elaborate, Catholic educators reflect together on their praxis—on their experience of doing Catholic education. This is theological reflection by the group on the Catholic education story.[9] A theology of revelation that holds that God continues to reveal himself through experience—that is, through the personal, social and situational events of one's

---

[9]   James E. Hug, SJ, ed., *Tracing the Spirit* (New York/Ramsey: Paulist Press, 1983). See the Introduction, p. 7, where he defines theological reflection as "reflection on experience understood in the light of religious experience by involved communities moving toward conversion and/or action." In my model of formation, these essentials for theological reflection are certainly all present: a group of Catholic educators reflecting critically on their vocation as Catholic educators; retelling the Christian story in light of their practice of Catholic education; with the purpose of strengthening their resolve and effectiveness as Catholic educators.

life—is essential to this notion of theological reflection. Thus, theological reflection, as a way of doing theology, must pay attention to the individual's experience and to the group's experience.

In his analysis of theological reflection, Thomas Clarke underscores the critical importance of memory (remembering) and the way in which memory must be brought to bear on the contemporary experience of a group's life and activities.[10] As a group reflects on the present moment of its experience, it must be very mindful of the past. It is memory that keeps the person and the group in touch with the key moments of the past. For reflection on present experience in the light of faith, it is the memory of Jesus and his liberating words and actions that make Jesus' prophetic words and healing actions present. Memory thus renders the past present, and it does so through story and story-telling.

> And as it is the sharing of the remembered story which ritually reconstitutes the Church, so it is by way of sharing stories, individual and communal, that the community engaged in theological reflection in any sector of its life and ministry is energized.[11]

Theological reflection on the Catholic education story, then, takes place by sharing personal and communal stories, and it is these stories shared by reflective Catholic educators that help constitute the Catholic education story.

An authentic Catholic education story is told by committed teachers, conscious of the vocational dimension of their role as Catholic educators and sincerely interested in evangelizing—in

---

[10] Thomas Clarke, "A New Way: Reflecting on Experience," in *Tracing the Spirit,* ed., James E. Hug, SJ, pp. 22-23.

[11] *Ibid.*, p. 23.

sharing their own experience of Jesus with their students. The Catholic education story is told especially through witness, through actions of compassion and forgiveness. But the story is related, too, in a critical, evangelizing education, an education that questions and challenges the assumptions of the dominant ideology in any society in light of the gospel. Essential to the story is an acknowledgement of the cross and a readiness to admit that sometimes there are no neat answers; that the only thing one can do is to wait patiently in hope, thereby giving oneself over to the mystery which is life.

It is the struggle to live this Catholic education story that teachers, both committed and experienced, and those new to Catholic education, reflect on together in the model of formation I am proposing. The shared reflection on the Catholic education story becomes a formative moment because of the sacredness and uniqueness of each person's story. And this act of reflecting and sharing in faith is indeed "a two way street"—as the teachers evangelize and form one another.

* * *

In these last four chapters I have identified and presented different theological, cultural and educational foundations operative in the model of formation I am about to describe in Part Three. It was important to situate the mission of the Catholic school within the overall mission of the church. It was important, too, to understand the frustration Catholic educators may experience when church leadership and structures are authoritarian and paternalistic rather than communitarian and empowering. I proposed evangelization as a foundation because my own vision of Catholic education is so inspired by Paul VI's theology of evangelization. And since the mission of Catholic education— evangelization— is done in a concrete time and place, it was necessary to look at our culture and the crises of the English Canadian church: the crisis of meaning, the crisis of authority, the crisis of modernity and the crisis of understanding. I concluded that the attitude of and skills for interpretation are more and more essential for doing Catholic education in our time. By way of digression, I explored further my own pastoral-theological journey as a Catholic educator. I found the image of a *wintry season* to be an apt metaphor to appreciate the difficulties and complexity, as well as the moments of hope, that are part and parcel of ministering in our contemporary English Canadian church. Finally, I explained some of the methodological dynamics I structure into the model of formation: the meaning of formation; formation as adult learning; and my understanding of theological reflection on the Catholic education story.

In Part Three, finally, I present a formation experience that is practical, relevant and rooted in the life and rhythm of the Catholic school. It is this experience, I believe, that can serve as a model of formation for any Catholic school or for any concerned group of Catholic educators.

Part Three
The Model

**Reflections
from a formation journal**

VI

Introduction
to a Formation Experience

"It seemed in every session our discussion eventually returned to life at school. What better way, then, of preserving the Catholic character? We constantly tied ideas to the practical and to the work at school . . . and to exploring different situations. We seemed most comfortable with the practical application and always seemed to come away with a feeling of hope. We shared ideas, situations and reflected on them. I can't think of a better way of engaging in the struggle to preserve the Catholic character of our school" (Joseph, a guidance counsellor).

A significant formation experience would make it possible for Catholic educators to become aware and to continue to be aware of the doing of Catholic education. This same formation experience would work at providing Catholic educators with the understanding, solidarity in community, and shared reflection on the practice of Catholic education that would allow them to meet the responsibilities of their vocation as Catholic educators. I believe the formation experiences that now exist, while necessary and valuable, are inadequate to meet the challenges and promises of this moment in Catholic education. Another model is called for.

The essence of the model of formation I propose is a reflection-group experience of ten Catholic high school educators which took place at a moderate-sized Catholic high school (1,250 students) in southern Ontario. They met two hours each month over eight months. Half of the group was made up of "beginning" teachers. The other half was constituted by committed, experienced Catholic teachers.

In the model I was especially concerned with the formation of the beginning teacher. "Beginning teacher" is understood here to mean someone with no more than three years of teaching experience. In choosing the beginning teacher, the invitational quality of the experience was accented. There were only five teachers on staff who could be designated *beginning*. Upon invitation, all five agreed to participate in the group. After a couple of weeks, however, one teacher declined. She offered lack of time as the reason, explaining that her professional life and personal life needed all of her time and attention. In the last days of June, however, a beginning teacher was transferred to the school and readily accepted the invitation to participate in the group.

Selecting the *committed, experienced Catholic teacher* was a more complex process. How does one define *commitment* in talking about *a committed Catholic educator*? I don't believe that there is an inflexible definition, but one might still offer a picture of a committed Catholic educator. I suggest the following characteristics:

- one who values and respects the students and other teachers as persons;

- one who is relatively happy and at ease with one's role as a Catholic educator;

- one whose love for the gospel and the spirit and teaching of the gospel is manifest;

- one who is not visibly uneasy in talking about faith or in putting her/his faith into action;

- one who worships regularly in the Roman Catholic Christian community and acknowledges that this moment of communal prayer is important in her/his life;

- one who teaches or evangelizes in very "unchurchy" ways; e.g., sharing one's own story of being a follower of Jesus;

- one who is critical, including self-critical; ready to question and able to see through much of the taken-for-grantedness of societal, educational and ecclesiastical structures.

The purpose of this project was to come up with a credible, doable, affordable, enriching formation experience for teachers in the Catholic high school. My idea was that over a period of time the conversation that would take place between beginning and more experienced Catholic teachers on the issues and questions (the content and context) of teaching in the Catholic high school would prove to be a valuable formation experience for the beginning teacher. At the same time, my hope was that this conversation would continue to challenge and form the experienced, committed teachers. The ongoing formation dimension to the model, while not the primary focus, was certainly important.[1]

---

[1]   The life and work of the reflection group was designed especially to avoid a we/they, formator/formatee split. The unity of the experience was emphasized: ten Catholic educators reflecting together on the ministry of teaching today in the Catholic high school. It is at the point of sharing one's story as a Catholic educator that the beginning teacher is able to discern and hopefully appropriate different aspects of the vision, values and attitudes of Catholic education.

In the group I served as facilitator and recorder. In a sense, I reprised the role of eavesdropper that I played in my earlier study, *On Evangelization in the Catholic High School.* From the conversation that ensued over eight months, I listened, assessed and recorded the spirit, insights, technical dynamics and practical wisdom emanating from the teachers. This is the stuff of my journal, and it is the stuff that makes such a conversation a practical, relevant model of formation for both beginning and experienced teachers in any Catholic school. And this is the stuff—the insights, dynamics, and practical wisdom—that I now report on.

In Chapter 7, I look at the teachers as they look at themselves as Catholic educators, and I record how it is that they understand *Catholic* and what it means for them as a teacher in a Catholic school. The focus for Chapter 8 is very much shaped by the conversation in Chapter 7: to be Catholic today is to experience more than a little societal and ecclesial complexity and ambiguity. So, how does one make sense of it all? How does one make meaning of it as a Catholic educator? My fundamental conviction is that the Catholic educator needs to appropriate the spirit of and master the skills for *interpretation.* In Chapter 8, then, I report on the conversation that takes place around the interpretation question, and I suggest ways in which interpretation itself can be understood as evangelization. In Chapter 9, I evaluate the conversation that is this formation experience: what are the possibilities—what is the potential for such a model of formation, and what implications could this model of formation have for publicly funded Catholic schools.

The immediate task now is to introduce the conversation and the participants who carry on the conversation. I begin with a review of some of the basic assumptions that are fundamental to my notion of formation. Next, I introduce the participants, establish the framework for the conversation and expand on some of the organizational and relational dynamics of the group experience. Then, the core of this chapter is the introduction to the experience itself. I will do this by reporting on the content and exchange that took place in the first two sessions of the formation conversation. Finally, I conclude the chapter with a brief commentary on five different themes emerging in the conversation, themes that pertain in an essential way to the formation experience.

Basic Assumptions

In Chapter 2 I identified and described some of my own theological assumptions in working out this particular model of formation. I find the theology of evangelization as articulated by Paul VI in his 1975 exhortation *On Evangelization in the Modern World* to be a most appropriate, relevant and challenging way to express the mission of Catholic education in Ontario in the mid-1990s. Certainly, there are other approaches and other philosophical foundations on which to focus, but my own theological vision for Catholic education finds meaning and relevancy in the critical function of evangelization proposed by Paul VI.

There are many questions one could examine in a formation experience for teachers in the Catholic high school. One is, however, necessarily limited by time: thus the decision to have eight two-hour sessions. I believe, though, that one is called by the demands, the needs that surface in the present-day reality of teaching in the Catholic high school: thus the proposal to emphasize interpretation and the acquiring of skills and strategies for interpretation as urgent content for teacher formation.

My understanding of formation is a third assumption, which I developed in Chapter 5. Formation is not indoctrination; it is not a teacher-centred process intended to dispense dogmatically correct answers. My meaning of formation is to reflect, in the context of community, on the experience of teaching in a Catholic high school; to listen respectfully to one another and God's Word; to support and challenge each other in the sharing of personal stories, struggles and questions. While I intend this formation experience primarily for beginning teachers, and therefore emphasize initial formation, my assumption is that ongoing or permanent formation takes place for the experienced teachers.

There are two further assumptions touched on in Chapter 1 that I would like to underline here in summary form as I describe this formation experience. In Catholic education in Ontario in the mid-1990s, there is a serious crisis regarding the preparation of teachers to teach in the Catholic high school. Even though there are formation experiences that are both necessary and valuable, I feel that they are insufficient to meet the challenge and vocational demands of the Catholic teacher. Secondly, my assumption is that there is this *vocation* dimension to teaching in the Catholic high school. But if there is no acknowledgement or ownership of the call, then there is no vocation. I see formation as an awakening to a vocation as a Catholic educator. Ongoing formation is a deepening of the ownership and commitment to one's vocation to teach in the Catholic high school.

The Participants

This very practical, *in situ* formation experience took place from September, 1991 to April, 1992 in a Catholic high school in southern Ontario. The ten participants—five beginning teachers and five experienced, committed teachers—met once a month in conversation on the vocation of teaching in the Catholic high school. To have a fuller appreciation of who the teachers are and what the experience is about, I present some identifying background data on each of the participants.

The Beginning Teachers:

Michael —   31 years old; 3 years of teaching experience; accounting and economics;

Mario —   26 years old; 3 years of teaching experience; business and accounting;

Marie —   25 years old; 2 years of teaching experience; mathematics and computer science;

Marisa —   28 years old; 1 year of teaching experience; science;

Gregory —   36 years old; 3 years of teaching experience; English.

The Experienced Teachers:

Raymond — 44 years old; 24 years of experience; religious studies;

Joseph —   48 years old; 24 years of experience; guidance;

Ann —   52 years old; 17 years of experience; family studies;

Arthur —   40 years old; 17 years of experience; mathematics and science;

Donna —   39 years old; 16 years of experience; business and guidance.

Additional Data on the Participants:

- There are 80 teachers on the faculty of this school. While teachers do know each other, there are varying degrees of knowledge and friendship. This is the case, as well, with the ten participants.

- Three of the participants are graduates of the high school. References to their student days then, and how it is now, sometimes slip into the conversation.

- Four of the beginning teachers have taken the OECTA Religion Course: Part One; one was in the process of taking it.

- The five experienced teachers are married and have established families. Three of the beginning teachers are married; one has children.

- Three of the five experienced teachers have been at the school for more than 15 years. One experienced teacher came four years ago from outside the province, and the other came from the elementary panel of another school board four years ago.

The Structure of the Experience

My role as facilitator of the experience was to constitute the group and propose an initial agenda regarding format, content for reflection and group dynamics. It was agreed that I would keep a journal of the group's reflections, questions, struggles and hopes. It is from this journal that I extracted the very practical and insightful data that makes up the essence of this formation experience: the personal and theological "stuff" from which I propose this experience as a model of formation for teachers in Catholic schools.

The following themes were approved by the group as the pertinent issues on which they would reflect:

- **Social analysis:** a critical look at the social and cultural factors that help shape both students and teachers;

- **Individualism:** as a strong characteristic element of our culture;

- **Catholic culture today:** what is it to be a Catholic in English Canada?; how do we experience "being Catholic" in our roles as Catholic teachers?;

- **Evangelization:** how do we live and teach the gospel—the Good News of Jesus Christ—in our Catholic school?;

- **Interpretation:** how do we arrive at a decision or a course of action to take in a social and ecclesial environment where there seem to be so many competing and conflicting values or ideas?;

- **Formation:** what does it mean to form teachers (both beginning and ongoing formation) for their ministry in Catholic education?;

- **A free session:** to further reflect on one of the above themes or pursue a new question;

- **Evaluation:** a review and assessment of the reflection sessions as a formation experience.

For each session I selected preparatory readings for the group, readings which touched on the theme being considered. The readings served as background and stimulus for the reflection experience.

Perhaps even more important were the reflection questions accompanying the readings. The questions attempted to connect the thought and ideas of the readings to the lived experience of the participant, both on the personal level and in one's role as Catholic educator. Framing these questions was part of my responsibility as facilitator, and I took considerable time at it. It was my hope that the questions would be the instrument that would allow the individuals in the group to dig reflectively into their own life experience as Catholic educators. For this retrieval of life experience data, I believed that the questions had to be carefully formulated.

As facilitator, I also prepared the prayer to begin the sessions. The ten-minute prayer segment served to relax the participants and connect what they were doing with Jesus' Word in the gospel and with their own call to be Catholic educators. The prayer reflections, for the most part biblical or from key church documents, were chosen in view of the theme. Usually one or two references to the prayer would be made during each discussion, which indicated to me both the importance of the prayer and the wisdom in beginning each session with prayer.[2]

During the sessions, I was the facilitator-recorder. I would move the discussion to the next question at the appropriate time. Sometimes I would pose a clarifying question or invite a person who was saying little to express an opinion or thought. Generally, I was very conscious of my role as listener.

Each session was evaluated in the final ten minutes. A particular aspect of the experience was examined by means of a brief oral evaluation; for example, quantity/quality of readings, the comfort level of the group or the quality of the exchange. A more detailed written evaluation was given to each participant to be returned a few days later.

Each two-hour session yielded ninety minutes of taped transcript. I made transcription notes as the reflection unfolded so that I could more easily identify speaker and input. As observer, I also made notes of both the verbal and nonverbal clues that would inject extra or particular meaning into the conversation. This is the personal and theological data that constitute my formation journal, and I draw from this journal to describe a fascinating yet practical formation experience.

---

[2]   In Appendix 1 I include the complete list of readings for each of the sessions as well as a sample set of reflection questions and a sample prayer reflection.

An Introduction to the Experience

Session 1: Social Analysis

Social analysis was the theme for the first reflection-sharing session. There were two reasons for beginning with social analysis. First, it was relatively non-threatening and, therefore, easier content to get into, as everyone has thoughts and opinions on social and cultural questions. Secondly, it allowed the teachers to look more closely at the context in which Catholic education at the high school takes place. The latter reason was the more critical of the two. Education does not take place in a vacuum. There is a very definite time, place, culture and social setting. The session was designed to investigate in more depth some of the factors that shape the social context. For the teacher-participants, there were two main perspectives to consider as they prepared for the session:[3]

1.   What is the impact of society on the students? How does the social context form the students, shaping their attitudes and behaviour?

2.   What are the pressures that come to bear on teachers today because of the difficult social and cultural climate?

The following are the principal themes selected from the participants' social analysis:

- the rapid pace of life;
- lack of commitment;
- broken families and brokenness in families;
- self-centredness;
- women's issues: violence towards, lack of respect for, lack

---

[3]   The preparation consisted in the background readings for the session and the set of reflection questions.

of equality, problems of women and men relating;

- home, values and instability;
- the openness and awareness of our students;
- the vulnerability of teens;
- how teachers are like students vis-à-vis society: they can't help but be influenced and shaped by social and cultural values;
- the need to critique and interpret social experience.

The source of my comments on this first session is my formation journal. As I have noted, I kept the journal to monitor the dynamics within the group and, more importantly, to log pieces of evidence that reveal the formation (or absence thereof!) taking place in the experience. In addition, I was soon to discover that the oral and written evaluations done by the teacher-participants after each session were to be equally effective instruments for measuring the quality of the formation.

From: Journal—Session 1

At first there were silent gaps . . . . The experienced teachers took the lead. There were some very good, genuine laughs, a sign of the easiness within the group. I noticed attentive, respectful listening throughout. In terms of content, the experienced teachers did most of the talking. There was a tendency to apply questions and responses (the responses to the set reflection questions) to a concrete school situation. As they talked about experience over the years with Grade Nines and Grade Twelves I noticed a genuine learning situation: the younger, inexperienced teachers were very attentive. I also noticed some deliberate, structured ideas (key points being made intentionally) in some of the interventions by the experienced teachers. This was not blatant, but finely nuanced. The older teachers would more often tap different aspects of their experience, often referring to their own children in citing examples. I noticed the attention in the eyes of the younger teachers listening.

Further in the journal I noted certain tendencies, questions or themes that took on meaning or seemed to have great relevance for the group:

- There were at least three interventions describing and focusing on the need to interpret our social and cultural context.

- A strong theme (perhaps 20 minutes of the 90-minute session) was that of women's issues.

- There was a real tendency for the teachers to apply the discussion almost immediately to the school situation. This was not a discussion for its own sake; everything was pretty practical.

Finally, in the journal I made note of what I had to work at or change:

- The use of scripture for prayer must be incorporated into the session. Prayer for the first session was simply a piece of reflective music by David Haas.

- There is a need for a more structured evaluation. I used only a general "What did you think of the session?" oral evaluation (and I had to depend on my notes to record the evaluations as I mistakenly turned off my tape recorder!)

- I was to find out at the end of Session 2 that there were too many readings.

- It was also evident that I had to be more clear and precise in phrasing the preparatory reflection questions.

This is but a brief overview of the first session. As a sketch it is quite incomplete. I do believe, however, that this overview is useful to introduce the formation-experience as a whole, its flow and proper dynamic, and some of the elements that must be considered in the analysis and interpretation of the data emerging from this initial experience. I was quite taken with the sincerity of the group and the quality of the reflection and sharing on social analysis. But even more critical for me was the fact that I was beginning to understand how formation was operative in this encounter and to discern some of the signs that teaching and learning (formation) was taking place as the participants formed one another.

Session 2: A Reflection on Individualism

The reflection-sharing session on individualism followed logically from the more general social analysis discussion of *Session 1*. My journal entry for *Session 2* is rich in observations on the content and dynamics of this second session. The following describes well some of the difficulties and benefits of this practical model for formation.

1. Major disappointment: three younger teachers were absent but with good cause. Marisa was sick all week; Marie had to coach two basketball teams; and Gregory had a school newspaper deadline. The disappointment was that they were three beginning teachers: "What would this do to the experience as a formation experience?" And even at the end of the evening there was disappointment for a different reason: the session had been so rich and engaging, and they had missed it. As the days progressed I was less bothered by their absence, figuring that the session was so beneficial. The evaluation helped a great deal.

2. I was very pleased with the prayer for this session. The scripture and reflection were chosen to enlighten and give some depth of understanding and focus to the themes: cooperation/community and competition/ individualism. I was

happy throughout the session with the references to the scripture and readings.

3. The evaluation process for this session was probably the most significant learning for me. I remembered to keep the tape playing for the oral evaluation, and I had prepared a written evaluation. Thus far I have received five of the seven. The evaluation really does highlight the learning that takes place.

4. For 10 to 15 minutes after the session Donna (an experienced teacher) chatted with Mario (a beginning teacher). During the session he was mostly silent, but in this conversation he was very animated and positive about the evening.

5. I intervened a few times this evening: a couple of times when invited to explain or clarify the meaning of a question; at other times to direct the discussion in certain areas. I believe these interventions were positive and important.

6. There is a good comfort level in the group. This comes out in the evaluation. Again there was some good-natured kidding and some easy laughs.

7. I noticed, too, several instances of expressive non-verbal communication: beginning teachers agreeing with what an experienced teacher was saying.

8. There was an especially rich use of story and anecdote in this session:
   - farm community;
   - ethnic community;
   - fences in backyards;
   - blizzard of 1977;
   - references to recent news reports.

9. Donna, an experienced teacher, was especially sensitive to

and very encouraging and affirming of the beginning teachers.

10. The theme *interpretation* came up again in this session, especially the challenge to interpret the struggle that is Catholic education; to call to mind the gospel values that challenge self-centredness.

11. The evaluations show that the group really appreciated the theme and thought that it was relevant. The prayer and the evaluation were important elements in the structure of the evening.

12. Emerging themes and questions:

   • interpretation;

   • the question of *time*: how to make time for such an experience. This is certainly more a question for beginning teachers because of the stress and pressure on them;

   • naming or identifying Catholic education as *struggle* seems to be emerging as a major theme: the struggle is the tension or gap that exists between the ideal and the lived reality.

13. *A question*: how to be sure that beginning teachers will not be intimidated by, or in too much awe of, the ease and contribution of the experienced teachers.

Commentary

From this analysis of *Sessions 1* and *2*, there are five comments to make or conclusions to draw which I believe are helpful in interpreting the formation elements in this group experience.

1. *Formation should be understood as both initial and ongoing.*

The fact that only two beginning teachers were present for *Session 2* was at first very disappointing for me.[4] I had envisaged the experience as forming young, inexperienced teachers first and experienced teachers second. Initial formation was privileged. I had to work through the questions of intention (initial/ongoing) and numbers (absences). The evaluations from *Session 2* and the subsequent sessions, including the final evaluation, were very helpful in this regard, as they highlighted the value of the experience for each participant. The reflection-sharing sessions on the vocation of the Catholic educator were very much like Thomas Groome's "two-way street." Even though there were only two inexperienced teachers present, formation happened, as the teachers present evangelized one another. I have the impression that over the course of the sessions the experienced teachers enjoyed the sessions more and may have benefited more from the experience because they had more time. (Generally, experienced staff are not as harried or hurried in school, having mastered routines, preparations and schedules.)

---

[4]   Generally, attendance at these sessions was good:

Session 1: all present;
Session 2: 3 beginning teachers absent;
Session 3: 1 beginning teacher absent;
Session 4: 1 experienced teacher absent;
Session 5: 1 beginning teacher absent;
Session 6: 2 beginning teachers and 1 experienced teacher absent;
Session 7: 1 beginning and 1 experienced teacher absent;
Session 8: all present.

One experienced teacher was away from school for two months due to illness. The other cases were consistently conflicts with other responsibilities. The interest was high, however, among the group itself and in their work. In several cases, those who could not make the session wrote out their reflections unsolicited and submitted them to me.

And necessarily, they have not only had more experience in teaching, but a more varied experience because their working context has been *Catholic* education. After several days of pondering the meaning of *intention* and *numbers* and *formation*, I began to feel confident that the sessions were *both* a *formation* for beginning teachers and an *ongoing formation* for the experienced.

2. *For such a formation experience, time is of the essence for beginning teachers.*

Over the eight sessions, as I have already indicated, beginning teachers were absent more frequently than experienced teachers. By saying this I in no way mean to question the sincerity or level of commitment of the beginning teachers. But given the pressures they are under—pressures that are part and parcel of starting out in the education profession—the sessions could become for them one more ball to juggle or one more meeting to fit in or one more "thing to do" in their already frenetically busy days. There were times when extra-curricular responsibilities had to take priority over the session. *Time*—the time to reflect and share—is a real problem: there is not enough of it. The dilemma for this model of formation or for any type of reflection on the meaning of Catholic education is that there is not sufficient time. For beginning teachers in particular, fresh out of the theorizing and visioning done in the faculties of education, there is just too much *doing* in their early years, with little built-in time for reflecting on what it is they are doing and why. There is something fundamentally wrong with this approach.

3. *Telling stories and relating first-hand experiences by way of examples are privileged instruments for adult learning.*

Stories are, as well, a very beneficial way to go about theological reflection and formation. *Story* figures prominently in *Session 2* and, indeed, became the means par excellence of sharing one's faith, values and strategies for evangelizing in subsequent sessions. I will develop this in some detail in the following chapter.

4. *How to be sure that beginning teachers will not be intimidated or too much in awe at the easiness and contribution of the older teachers?*

This question arose out of *Session 2* and remained a preoccupation for the first four sessions. Reasons for intimidation (unintentional, to be sure) are clear: general differences in age; the more vast amount of professional "history" the experienced teachers had to reflect on and draw from. The nature of this model of formation is to reflect on experience. It follows, then, that there might be an initial reluctance for the beginning teachers to share, given that their experiences are fewer and tend to be less varied. My observations, however, lead me to believe that beginning teachers can overcome their initial reluctance to share. First of all, confidence comes with time and familiarity, that is, with experience. By *Session 5,* there was no longer this intimidation or reluctance. Beginning teachers were sharing as much and as frequently as experienced teachers. Secondly, the confidence level of the beginning teacher can be boosted by the affirming and encouraging gestures, smiles or words of the experienced teacher—without it being patronizing. This was the strategic role Donna was to play with the beginning teachers throughout the sessions. And thirdly, while facilitation should be unobtrusive, there can be a right time to invite comment or opinion from different participants. Sensitivity is needed to avoid embarrassing or putting anyone on the spot. A certain reluctance to share on the part of the inexperienced teachers is natural at the beginning of the experience. The critical challenge for all participants in the reflection process is to get beyond this reluctance.

5. *Catholic education is struggle.*

There were suggestions in the first two sessions that to speak about Catholic education and the ideals embodied in any philosophy or theology of Catholic education is to speak of *struggle*. The struggle theme as a description of Catholic education is woven throughout the entire experience. Raymond underscores the struggle dimension in his observation that Catholic schools are as much caught up with the promotion of individualism and competition as are public schools. From my journal entry for *Session 2:*

> I don't think a sense of community and cooperation, like that in the gospels, is at the centre of our education. I think we're struggling to make it that way. I think the Catholic high school, until recently anyway, has basically catered to academic-stream kids . . . who would get a good preparation for university. In many ways it reinforces the competitiveness.

Joseph recognizes the possibility that a Catholic education can be different because of the ideals at the heart of our mission statements. But he wonders if the future will have enough Catholic educators engaged actively in the struggle to interpret what is going on in education in terms of gospel values:

> I think to a great extent our ideas are there . . . the mission statement, etc. At the idea or intellectual level we are there . . . but the questions are: how much is that? And how much do we make this an operative thing within our schools? We're talking here about interpretation: do we interpret what we are doing in terms of gospel values? This is the real struggle! . . . . Are we going to have Catholic educators to keep on interpreting experience in terms of the gospel values so that there is a meaning for why we do things like this?

Catholic education really takes place in the gap; that is, in the struggle area, between the ideals of the vision statements and the lived reality of the corridors, classrooms and cafeteria. Being a privileged observer to the ongoing conversation between Catholic educators on the meaning of their vocation has confirmed for me the truth of the intuition that the element of struggle must be central to any description of Catholic education.

In the preceding pages, I have presented the bare bones of a model of formation for teachers in a Catholic school—a model that is at once practical and relevant; that is, a model based on practice, on the content and rhythm of everyday school life; and a model that intends to be a formative experience for both beginning and experienced teachers. Conversation is really at the heart of this model. Through a series of conversations in a reflection group made up of beginning and experienced teachers, teachers evangelize and form one another. The themes for reflection are rather eclectic. In this experience the teachers were receptive to my particular interests, but for such a model to work, I believe, any theme will do as long as it is pertinent to the questions and issues of Catholic education, allows teachers to get in touch with their own everyday experience, and helps shed light on what it means to teach in a Catholic school today.

In the next two chapters I enflesh the bones of this model of formation. I do so, first, by replaying a conversation that explores what it means to be Catholic and to teach in the Catholic environment today. Secondly, I present a report of a conversation on the importance of interpretation—on the spirit of and skills for interpretation—in our evangelizing efforts today in the Catholic school.

VII

The Catholic Teacher in the 1990s: Personal Faith and Professional Mission

"I think we're in the gray area in-between seasons. We're leaving one season and coming into a new season" (Marisa, science teacher).

"I see the seasons from the point of view of our prayer and Ecclesiastes *and 'the time for keeping and the time for throwing away' and also 'a time for knocking down and a time for building.' What are we going to keep, and what are we going to go on with, and what are we going to leave behind because we have outgrown it?"* (Ann, family studies teacher).

"I am more like Ann and Ecclesiastes: 'A time for healing and a time for searching.' The end of winter and into spring: renewal and starting fresh" (Donna, business teacher).

Catholic Culture Today was the third topic proposed for the reflection-sharing sessions. For Catholic education to be authentic and effective, teachers must attend to what it means to be Catholic in our time and place. As Catholic educators, the teachers are expected to evangelize—to invite students to come to know, love and follow Jesus; and as members of the Catholic community, the teachers invite students to follow Jesus as part of the Roman Catholic Christian community. It is important, then, for a formation experience, that teachers reflect on what it is and what it means to be Catholic: personally, what gives them meaning? What enriches them? What frustrates them?

I begin my report on this segment of the teachers' conversation with several observations of a technical nature on the structure and functioning of this particular formation model. I then select four themes central to teaching in a Catholic school today and offer a brief analysis of each. The foundations elaborated in Part Two, I believe, are helpful in understanding the significance of these themes. At the same time, the experience or practice of the teachers adds further meaning and relevance to these same theoretical foundations. Finally, I offer three comments on different aspects of this formation experience that I feel are beneficial for strategizing on the way we do Catholic education.

Some Comments on the Formation Experience

The discussion that follows is based on *Sessions 3* and *4* of the formation experience. *Session 3* was so engaging that the group opted to continue the reflection in *Session 4*. The model of formation I am proposing makes this possible by including a free session to be used according to the group's wants and needs. (Unfortunately, I am only able to highlight some of the data, exchange and learning dynamics that transpired in these sessions, because of restrictions of space. Of special interest is *The Theological Elements* document I created at the end of

Session 3. In this six-page document I have elaborated a *theology* from the reflections of the teacher-participants in the first session on Catholic culture. In fact, a sharing on this theology itself became the point of departure for the work in the second session on Catholic culture. I include this document as Appendix 2 because I feel it is an interesting example of doing practical theology around the Catholic education question. I feel, also, that it expands on and gives further colour to the faith journey of these Catholic educators.

The reflection on experience operative in *Session 3* is a reflection and sharing on what it means to be a Roman Catholic today. In terms of facilitating this reflection, the choice of background readings proved to be very beneficial.[1] Satisfaction with the readings was evident both in the evaluations at the end of the sessions, and more importantly, in the energy and enthusiasm the readings seemed to generate in the sessions themselves. The readings definitely gave content and focus to these sessions. In some instances, this was new content for the teacher-participants. They had not heard many of these concepts or perspectives before—or had not seen them put in this way. In other cases, while the contents were not new, the readings seemed to articulate well ideas and intuitions participants had been unable to express.

---

[1]   Readings for Sessions 3 and 4:

•   Jack Costello, SJ, "Towards an Adult Church," Compass (January/February, 1990), pp. 37-39.

•   Andrew M. Greeley, "Sacraments Keep Catholics High on the Church," National Catholic Reporter (April 12, 1991), pp. 12-13.

•   Elizabeth Johnson, CSJ, "Recovering Women's Faith Experience from the Scriptures," in Miriam's Song II (Hyattsville, Maryland: Priests for Equality), pp. 7-11.

•   Eugene Kennedy, "The Shape of Things to Come" in The Now and Future Church (Garden City, New York: Image Books, 1985), pp. 173-185.

The reflection questions for each session are intended to help the teachers mine some of the implications of their own practice and experience and to process the preparatory readings. A glance at the questions prepared for *Sessions 3* and *4* give some indication of the focus of the discussion and the type of sharing that took place:

1. Referring to Andrew Greeley's reasons for being and remaining Catholic, how would you answer that question?

2. Think of a symbol, an image, a metaphor that describes what it means to be Roman Catholic today.

3. What do you think are the essentials in being Roman Catholic today? Describe what you think *the Catholic reflex* is.

4. Of these essentials, which ones can we work at handing on to our students, especially to the unchurched kids in our schools?

5. Talk a bit about your idea of "the shape of things to come" (Kennedy's article).

6. What are your thoughts about the theology of the last session, *The Theological Elements* document? Do you feel this to be an accurate representation of our last reflection-sharing? What would you nuance, change, clarify? On what points do you find yourself most in agreement?

7. What about the Elizabeth Johnson article on feminist theology? What are your views, questions and insights? And connecting this with the struggle of women for equality in the church and in society, what should be our approach in the Catholic high school?

The readings and reflection questions together contributed greatly to making these two sessions a genuine experience in collaborative learning. The participants, both the experienced and beginning teachers, had strong views and feelings about what it is to be Roman Catholic today—views they readily shared. They were attentive to and respectful of each person's story, but at the same time, they were forceful in their own critique of certain institutional structures they deemed to be more obstacle than aid in living out the gospel.

The use of image and symbol served the formation experience of these sessions very well. For me as facilitator, this was new language and a new instrumentality for communication. It was new, too, for some of the participants. Yet it was accepted and used most creatively by the participants, often shedding new and different light on the theme or taking the question in a surprisingly different direction.

A Report on the
Catholic Teachers' Faith Journey

From the richness of the reflection-sharing on the topic *What it Means to Be Roman Catholic Today*, I select four themes that I feel are central, themes that shed some light on where the teachers find themselves in their own faith journey as Roman Catholics today. An analysis of these themes can serve as a vehicle, too, to enter into the minds, hearts and evangelizing strategies of these Catholic educators reflecting on their own practice and experience.

1. *Opting for a Community Model of Church over an Authoritarian Model of Church*

Jack Costello's article, "Towards an Adult Church," seemed to trigger a flood of pre-Vatican II church memories and stories for Joseph, Ann and Raymond. Their stories illustrated especially the patriarchal power structure of that church. In my journal for *Session 4* I note:

Some vivid anecdotes of the pre-Vatican II church experience: everyone went to Sunday Mass; altar boys recited incomprehensible Latin sayings; in some parishes people bought their own pews; there were never any questions raised or asked about the way things were; the difficult 1960s and the birth control controversy was a terrible dilemma for many young Catholic couples. I think that the relating of this experience helped both the beginning and inexperienced teachers to understand more the ways the authoritarian, patriarchal structures were operative in church life.

Jack Costello suggests that the transactional analysis model—the parent-child-adult paradigm—is applicable to the way Roman Catholics have regarded themselves in the church. The older teachers in particular were able to see themselves as *children*, not as *adults* in those pre-Vatican II years. Indeed, in too many instances, even today, there are vestiges of the domineering, patronizing *parent*—"from the pedestal of clericalism" as one teacher phrased it—which prevents adults from being and behaving like adult members of the church.

In my *Theological Elements* document from *Session 3* I wrote:

Marisa brings up the Newfoundland (sexual assault) experience. This was the point of departure for the sharing on "Towards an Adult Church." Marisa was in St. John's during the televised hearings. In the exchange at this point, a lot of parent/child discussion comes into play. Through stories and anecdotes they relate how they want to shuck off the child in them that accepts the parent-dictates of parent-clergy.

Ann tells this story: "This spring we visited our son in X-ville. His wife isn't Catholic, and I don't think B. has been going to Mass that regularly. But because we were coming he found out what time Mass was and indicated he was going to come with us. So we went to church, . . . and this priest . . . put down women, put down homosexuals; he attacked a couple of political parties, . . . and I think he also worked on new immigrants. And when we came out of church I was thinking and hoping maybe B. would go back again, . . . but why would you ever go back there? I wouldn't go back to that church! And I was thinking: "Did I have a responsibility to go up to this man—and he wasn't old, maybe 40—and tell him that I really disagree with what you said!" I didn't. But I was mad at myself after, that I really didn't have the guts to do it.

In both sessions on Catholic culture, there was a strong agreement that "We can't stand by anymore and let such priests get away with clerical abuses of power." The teacher-participants, recognizing their *adulthood*, were saying that they had to take ownership and accept responsibility in the church. They were acknowledging that their co-dependency allows such priests as Ann describes to dominate. At the same time, it was said that the institutional church which supports abusive structures has got to change. The teachers, drawing from their own diverse experiences, were resonating completely with the theological critiques of Rémi Parent and Leonardo Boff.

A nagging question throughout these reflections had to do with the relationship between faith and culture. The question can be phrased in this way: "How much of the pre-Vatican II faith was based on cultural phenomena; for example, the cultural respect accorded clergy, their role and the authority structure that supported that role? And, how much of that faith was deeper, a personalized and owned faith not dependent on such cultural structures?" I remarked in my journal for *Session 3:*

Another finding: the intertwining of faith and culture. It is becoming more and more clear to me that a real question is always going to be: "What is of faith and the gospel, and what is of the culture?" From the discussion, so much of what folks thought to be essential really proved to be cultural things that no longer work in a changing society and culture. And this brought them to the hermeneutical task: to interpret and to work at personal synthesis. That means both being suspicious of what we have learned, and yet, being ready to retrieve from our tradition what is essential. It is becoming more and more clear that these people anyway are no longer ready to allow the institution and hierarchy to do that task for them.

The hermeneutical task came very much into play in the reflection on Elizabeth Johnson's "Recovering Women's Faith Experience from the Scriptures." This discussion took place on December 6th, the anniversary of the Montreal massacre—a fact that added conviction and urgency to the sharing. Joseph, Michael, Ann and Marisa had this exchange on androcentrism in the church:

Joseph: That's androcentrism! Everything in the church is presented through the man's perception. I don't know about rights, but what happens is that your existence is defined through men's ideals and perceptions. The gospels are written through male eyes and by males.

Michael: But tell me, where do women have any less rights than I do in the church, outside of not being able to be a priest?

Ann: If you're part of a company—you're a junior executive or something—you work a lot and do a lot of work in the church, but the rules say that you, for some reason or other, can't take a prominent position and rise to the level of facilitator of the parish, for example. Then, that's discrimination. You're an unequal partner. That's what I feel.

Marisa: And when you look at the role of the clergy and the characteristics they have to have—to be that good role model—I mean . . . can't women bring a totally new dimension to that vocation? I mean . . . women have these qualities too! And at school, you instill in the kids you are teaching that women have to be self-sufficient nowadays, and you can't depend on men . . . and in society there is "equality." But you don't ever talk about the church! You try to tell them to take on a new role in society: don't be subservient to men; but you can't bring the church into that, which makes the church completely irrelevant.

Ann: It's not what Michael says. The question—it's a good question. But it's that he doesn't see the problem! That's what's so frustrating for women!

Michael: Why didn't this come up years ago?

Assorted voices: Look at the songs. Look at the marriage rite: "Honour and obey" (voices in unison!). Look at "Thou shalt not covet thy neighbour's wife!" It was all there!

In my journal for *Session 4* I commented on the sincerity and depth of this exchange:

In a sense, although we were continuing *Session 3* on Catholic culture today, the heart of the discussion really was the women's issue, which makes me believe for these Catholic educators and many others today that the women's issue is central to the problem of Catholic culture. As such, I think it was a terrific learning experience. The ideas and critical reflection developed gradually: from pride in having altar girls to questioning the exclusion of women from the priesthood to anger and frustration that women can't be expected to be treated equally in the church, consequently rendering the church irrelevant to many. Then there were insights and excitement in discovering androcentrism and how it works in the scriptures. There was the challenge that men should feel angry about the exclusion of their wives and daughters because of the sin of sexism. I really feel that this was a collaborative learning group. It was fascinating to watch the development: getting deeper and deeper into the question. The readings were very helpful. I believe each person came away with something new regarding their insights and feelings about faith and women.

The pre-Vatican II and post-Vatican II clericalism and androcentrism deeply rooted in our institutional structures are certainly signs of an authoritarian model of church. Mario's model is different, one based on community and participation:

> I can't take credit for this image of church. It sort of developed for me after taking the Religion Course—Part One. But the image we worked on was the community: a circular view of the people in the community and the priest in the centre as facilitator. The community is the church, with decision-making invested in the people, and the priest helping to bring it about. Instead of pyramid-style, things filtering down to the people, it is circular.

Mario's option for the circular, and his critique of the pyramidal imagery, evoke the critique made by Rémi Parent and Leonardo Boff, especially Boff's description of "Church as charism." It is decidedly the community model of church that the teacher-participants opt for, as we shall see in their reflection on sacramentality.

2. Catholics and the Sacraments

The teachers were in full agreement with Andrew Greeley's findings that Catholics remain in the church because the sacramental life of the church has too great a hold on them. From

Greeley's list of 13 reasons for remaining Catholic (see: Appendix 2: *Theological Elements*), the consensus was that "Catholic heritage," sacraments, and "a faith to pass on to their children" were the major reasons for being and remaining Catholic. Sacraments and the liturgy—both the personal and communal dimensions—would come up often as something personally rich and meaningful and to be treasured. For Donna, who entered fully into sacramental life only as an adult, faith is like the seasons: developing and changing; meaning different things at different times. The sacramental initiation of her children has given strength and meaning to her own faith:

> My faith is a lot like the seasons in the prayer we did. My faith changes as my life changes. Just this past Sunday there was the inscription service for the Grade-Twos at church, and that takes on new meaning for me: the first communion of my child. The sacrament is richer now. I didn't have a strong Catholic background. But with these moments . . . my hope is that my kids will have one. And this is a source of strength for me now . . . as my parents get older and as I go through different seasons. I believe that my faith will be a great help to me.

In the reflections on sacraments, great emphasis was placed on the sense of community and the importance of participation. Communal prayer and liturgy should be relevant, addressing the needs of the people and speaking to them "where they are at," especially the kids in the school. There is respect, too, for the sacred: for quiet and joy and celebration. Marie reflects back on liturgy during her college years:

> At college we had 10:00 p.m. Mass on Sundays. Dimmed all the lights. There was a real sense of community. It was a traditional or ordinary parish-type liturgy, but the students were all involved. It was an important thing for us to do Sunday night. It was the sense of community.

This appreciation for community and participation is the connecting point between those who experienced the pre-Vatican II church and those who know the church only in the last three decades. For the former, when liturgy is done well, it is freeing and enriching. For the latter, it is meaningful. For both, when there is an absence of community and participation, it is stifling, mediocre, boring and, at times, as in Ann's case, it leads to frustration and anger.

3.   *On the Essentials of Being a Roman Catholic Today . . . and the Catholic Reflex!*

Perhaps the most challenging problem facing Catholic educators today and in the future is the question of *the unchurched*, or, the nominal Catholic. Catholic kids are baptized and many are in Catholic schools, but many of them receive little faith education at home and have little or no contact with the parish. Then it is the school, as the Ontario Bishops have said, which becomes the primary place where these students experience the church as an alternative community. The question for the teachers was: "What can the school do for so many unchurched kids in our midst?" Raymond emphasized the centrality of community as a Catholic essential:

> If kids do not have access to a system of shared meaning, it is because we as the adult community are not providing it.

For Joseph, the "foundational essentials" were the initiation sacraments, baptism and Eucharist:

> Even the unchurched know they have been baptized and can go to communion. There will come a "searching-for-meaning" time later in adult life. Then they will go back to retrieve some of the meaning experienced at key moments in their early adolescent liturgical and sacramental life.

There were rich ideas, too, regarding *the Catholic reflex*, ideas that are consistent with sacramentality as the Catholic way of being, doing and looking at reality. It was this notion that was proposed by Langdon Gilkey and Andrew M. Greeley as the essential characteristic of Catholics. Regarding *the Catholic reflex*, the teachers made the following notes.

- It is changing. It still does kick in. It is being nurtured especially in liturgical and sacramental experiences.

- It manifests itself more often now in a faith that acts more than in a faith of the past that was simply passive and tried to avoid sin.

- There is a strong social justice face to the Catholic reflex.

- It sometimes does not surface until years later during the search for meaning.

- Signs and physical, cultural symbols are still important: icons, enthroned book of scriptures, candles.

- It is passed on by the force of personal witness and actions more than by lectures and words.

- When kids are vulnerable, this is a really teachable moment to pass on the Catholic reflex.

4. *The Catholic Environment Today Described in Terms of the Seasons*

The prayer for *Session 3* was thematic, based on the seasons and time in Ecclesiastes 3:1-8 and Jesus' foretelling his death and resurrection in John 12:20-28. As a prelude to the prayer, I commented that time and weather and climate can at times be useful metaphors to understand where we are at as individuals in life; and as a community, where we are at in the institutional life of the church. I asked them to keep this question in mind as they shared in the session: "What season do you think best reflects where we are at now as church?"[2] I leave it to the teachers to give their own ecclesial meteorological analyses and forecasts:

Joseph: I chose winter. Yeah, it struck me that we're in winter, because it seems to me: it's a conservative church and we're going to have to go in a new direction before too long. We're running out of priests as we know them. I have a friend in the States: his parish virtually hires the priest. They negotiate with the bishop for the kind of priest the parish feels it needs best. He was telling me a lot of parishes there have really become ideological parishes, a special focus and environment. People tend to drive quite a ways to get to such a parish. You're more comfortable; there is more meaning. Right now, I think, we're in a structure of the holding pattern of winter. I think a lot of things have gone on, and we are ready for some re-birth and new directions.

Arthur: Winter! I agree with Joseph. There are things that have to change or will change. When that change starts to happen, we'll call that spring. But I think that we're in that stage, the season before, and that's winter.

Marisa: I think we're in the gray area in-between seasons. We're leaving one season and coming into a new season.

Ann: Ecclesiastes and "the time for keeping and the time for throwing away" and also "a time for knocking down and a time for building." What are we going to keep, and what are we going to go on with, and what are we going to leave behind because we have outgrown it?

---

2   This idea was generated from the stuff of my own particular journey at the time. As I observed in Chapter 4, I had found Karl Rahner's *Faith in a Wintry Season* to be very helpful personally in terms of perspective for my own ministry. Wondering how other followers of Jesus—like Catholic educators—might describe our present ecclesial climate, I decided to ask the question. The image *season*, I soon discovered, was for me a wonderfully new way of tapping into the imagination. It provided a new language and, therefore, new ways of looking at the present reality of church life.

Raymond: I like Marisa's idea that we are kind of in-between. I put late winter-early spring. In the early spring you go out, and there are already some early shoots sticking up: the crocuses are out. The shoots push off the old dead leaves. But there is still snow all over the place. The way we are: there are a lot of problems, but the fresh shoots are pushing off the dead leaves. You can't keep them down. Young people and concerned laity are excited about the church and want to go in new ways. Early spring, though, is dangerous: buds and shoots can be stepped on by big boots!

Michael: It is hard to say. I have difficulty trying to grasp that concept. I guess, if anything, I can relate church to summertime. I don't really see a lot of changing going on. Summer weather is pretty constant, consistent, warm and breezy. I like it. It's a nice time of year. I don't see the church having a lot of changes right now. It's pretty consistent, and I can only speak of the parish that I am in. I like it. I think that it is still effective.

Gregory: To take a summer a bit further: the real hot spells would equate to the aspects of the church that have been under fire. But I also thought of the fall: the harvest moon. We do need changes, and that is the time of change, of harvest.

Marie: More spring, I feel. I think we are forced to make changes. We are not touching the younger people we need to touch, so changes will have to be made.

Donna: I am more like Ann and Ecclesiastes: "A time for healing and a time for searching." The end of winter and into spring: renewal and starting fresh.

Commentary

The preceding teachers' reflections on Catholic culture today, or their sense of the contemporary environment, give rise to three comments that I believe are helpful in interpreting their sharing, and showing the possible benefits of this process for Catholic education and how it serves as a formation experience for Catholic educators.

1.   There is a need to reclaim sacramentality

The data generated in these two sessions of reflection on Catholic culture confirm Andrew Greeley's thesis that in spite of the institutional scandals and structural weaknesses that seemingly should be obstacles to hanging tough in the church, Catholics generally don't leave the church, because they like it too much. And what they like about the church especially is the personal meaning afforded by their participation in the sacraments. Indeed, it seems that even knowing that the sacramental moment of awe and mystery is there when they need it gives Catholics sufficient reason to stay in the church. "Sacraments keep Catholics high on the church" is the way Greeley puts it. Perhaps it is Michael, of all the teachers, who best reflects the truth of Greeley's thesis that the Catholic imagination is more sacramental than dialectical:

> We have had some poor priests, too, where I go to church, and we still have some. But I never thought of it. I'm devout. I go every week. Some priests I don't like at all. I don't like their sermons. I tune out. And sometimes I leave Mass, and I don't feel much. I didn't listen to him. But I say to myself: "I didn't go to church to listen to the priest. I listen to the Mass! If I don't like the priest, I don't listen to him." I say to myself: "The church, going to Mass, is more to me than the human aspect of it." I read about the human aspects— that bothers me—but the church is more than human priests.

Michael isn't bothered that much by bad preaching or institutional scandals. He tunes the priest out. His faith is deeply personal and private. Michael is very much taken with the awe, the mystery, the moment of transcendence offered in the sacrament. He is taken, too, with Greeley's description and assessment of Catholics today: "I found it to be an excellent summary of what it means to be Catholic."

While I can argue with Michael's understanding of church and eucharist and his notion of the liturgy of the Word, I do believe he is on to something fundamentally important, rooting his faith-life so much in the sacrament. As I wrote in Chapter 3, as Catholics we need to reclaim sacramentality. I believe this to be especially urgent for Catholic education. If sacramentality is at the heart of Catholicism, and if the schools now are prime socializers of the students into church life, then we need new and creative ways of more effectively incorporating sacraments and the sacramental outlook and approach to life into the school.

The example of Michael clearly confirms Greeley's thesis, but I believe it also is evident from the above analysis of the teacher-participants' attitudes regarding the sacraments: all of them continue to anchor themselves firmly in the life of the church because of the church's sacramental life. If it is sacramentality that is the main source of meaning for Catholic educators, then surely our evangelization efforts and religious education programs should be reviewed in light of Greeley's findings. As I mentioned earlier, it is my experience and fear that we are too word-founded in our evangelization. We have overlooked the riches inherent in the Catholic imagination. I am convinced that this question needs further practical, theological attention on the part of Catholic educators.

2. An Example of the Beginning Teachers Forming the Experienced Teachers

In my journal for *Session 4* I caution myself:

> I really need to be alert to the *two* churches: pre-Vatican II
> and post-Vatican II. Some in the group refer to those two
> different experiences of church in the *child/parent* paradigm
> of transactional analysis. In a certain sense, at least coming
> out in this session, it is the children, the younger teachers,
> who feel more at home with the questioning spirit of the
> post-Vatican II church. In this session and in other sessions,
> the pre-Vatican II teachers refer to the struggle, the pain, the
> lack of freedom, the guilt that all seemed to be part of the
> pre-Vatican II church experience.

I believe that caution, in this instance, is the correct word. I have
to be careful, and other Catholic educators of my vintage with
still powerful memories of the pre-Vatican II church must be
careful too, not to impose upon younger teachers our own
agenda, especially if that personal agenda is charged with guilt,
anger and frustration.[3] There are enough causes for anger and

---

[3]   There is another side to this argument that should be made as well.
While we should not impose on the present our hang-ups from the past, I do feel
that it is important to make present to the post-Vatican II generations the positive
elements of the tradition that we have experienced but which now seem to have
become lost, neglected or set aside. The hermeneutical stance has to do with retrieval, and it must be undertaken by teachers with pre-Vatican II memory. There
are some traditions, signs, symbols and images that could be a source of rich
meaning for believers today: fasting, the use of processions in liturgy, pilgrimages, a renewed Way of the Cross, silence in retreats and days of reflection, some
saints whose lives and example speak in a relevant way to our time and place,
the meaning of Advent and Lent and the general rhythm of the liturgical year.
Many post-Vatican II Catholics have little or no sense of these traditional practices and symbols. And yet these things do constitute in a very concrete way the
Catholic imagination, and thus they are capable of carrying much meaning for
Catholics. This is an important instance of reclaiming sacramentality in the wider sense of the term.

frustration in the institutional church today without needlessly importing them from yesteryear. In the reflections, Marie comments on difficulties now experienced by pre-Vatican II folks in the present church:

> When I was taking my religion course, there were—how do I put it—older people and younger people, and the people who were pre-Vatican II said they had a hard time now because they are allowed to question things. Before you didn't question. You just followed and obeyed the law. They found it difficult that we are allowed to ask so many questions and wonder and work through it, and I've always been allowed to ask questions about my faith. It's me and part of me! But I can see that it is hard for a lot of people.

Looking at his own post-Vatican II experience, Gregory relates how he was introduced into the attitude of healthy questioning:

> I remember when I was in high school, that basically we were instructed that our faith will strengthen if we are questioning; that if you are not questioning, then you are not really doing much to be in touch with your faith. So it is a good thing to question. Definitely!

Marie's and Gregory's questioning stance is something positive and critically important for any formation experience. A questioning attitude makes one more comfortable with change, and, in the church today—in spite of the way it might appear—and in Catholic education, fundamental changes are taking place. I refer back to my journal for *Session 4:*

> Following on the "two churches" thought: more and more, the pre-Vatican II experience of church is going the way of the dodo bird! I qualify that by referring to teachers in Catholic schools. Obviously it is the case with the students we have. For some of the beginning teachers—both in the group and elsewhere—1965 is ancient history. What came out in today's discussion: more changes are definitely

needed. And we thought Vatican II triggered all of the changes that would be necessary! The changes must reflect the equality and the dignity of women in the church. And more, the changes must be structural—away from the hierarchical-patriarchal model to a more cooperative-communitarian model.

Perhaps Joseph captures best the urgency of the need to make fundamental changes with his reflection:

The church and the Catholic school must face change. It's inevitable: like a snowball going downhill. Look how many unchurched students we have now whose parents had some church! But fifteen years from now, these kids will be adults and parents. What faith, what church experience will they have? There's going to be a crisis point. There have to be changes.

3.   A Reflection on Story and Symbol and the Formation Experience

In my commentary on the introduction to the formation experience, I underscored the usefulness of *story* for sharing one's faith, values and evangelizing strategies. In Chapter 5, I developed my understanding of story as an educational foundation. I was helped by Thomas Clarke's observation that memory is essential for story: memory makes the past present through story. Clarke observed, too, that as memory is the way to the past, so imagination is the key to getting into the future. As story is the instrument of memory, so symbol and image are the instruments serving the imagination. It is the symbol or image that unlocks or frees the mind from a rigid, merely logical way of looking at reality. Packed into the symbol are layers of meaning and detail that likely would not surface, or would not surface as vividly, in a rational, linear description of an event.

In my journal for *Session 3,* I made note of the way story and symbol functioned in the formation experience:

> Special note should be made of the use of *anecdote* and *story*, of *images* and *symbols*. I found it especially rich that when they talked of the older church—the traditional church of their youth—they tended to tell *stories*. There were examples. Memory came into play. They understood some of the theology of that older church now in looking back at it. But that was a church for that time. The time and place were different. The society and culture were vastly different.

> However, when they begin to describe the church of the present and the future, I found that the use of *image* and *symbol* was a wonderful tool for them to theologize, perhaps in ways that they did not think they were capable of. This became very clear in reflections on a symbol for the church today and the season they think the church is in today. A real finding is the possibility of *symbol* and *image* as ways of getting at one's feeling and thoughts and getting into one's personal pilgrimage as Christian.

I conclude this discussion of the teachers' reflections on Catholic culture by referring once more to the *Theological Elements* document of *Session 3* and the analysis and interpretation of the teachers' use of *symbol* or *image* to describe what it means to be Roman Catholic today.

> Arthur: Does this make any sense: something like you're out on the ocean. I like being on water. So you are out there floating around, but eventually you want to get back to land. I think there are a lot of Catholics these days who are asking a lot of questions, searching, looking around. They are not really sure about their faith, but it's there, and you can

always go back to it. I don't know: you're adrift on the ocean, but you can always go back to it.

Theological Elements: Arthur describes the free-floating situation of many Catholics today, but at the same time he sees *church* and *faith* (not always distinct) as land: "solid" and "constant," a place to come home to. The meaning seems to be that church is more faith and sacramental experience. Church makes meaning for people. It is not church in the hierarchical or institutional structure.

Joseph: The image I have: I saw it in terms of building a house you know. I saw . . . kind of the church as foundation, and in the past—like for my parents—it was the whole house, and there were rooms that were set, things that you were supposed to believe in. Everything was set. And you just moved into the house and lived there, and you lived in the rooms as they were set. Where . . . my church . . . I still think I have the same foundation, but all the materials are lying around, and I have some real serious input into the way that church is going to be. And if I want to set it up that way; if I want to use what the church has to offer me; if I want to use the sacraments in a way that will be helpful to me; if I want to use clergy for interpretation and help, then I'll use them that way. But Catholics should be able to structure their own . . . on that foundation. They should be able to structure their own rooms and structure their own passageways so that it kind of is their own faith within a general structure. I grew up believing that there are certain dogmas, certain truths that are stable. But there is a whole interpretation of how we apply this to our lives and so forth. I really see a creative element that is part of our faith.

Theological Elements: Joseph's image is a house. We have the pre-Vatican II and post-Vatican II churches in relief. Foundation is important, but then, so is an adult putting together of the synthesis. Here, too, the *adult/parent* paradigm is operative and useful for understanding both church and faith. Throughout Joseph's image is the personal ownership and interpretation that are necessary. There is very much a creative dimension to believing today and to membership in the church.[4]

Raymond: It's hard trying to think of an image. I guess for me it's more the community, the struggling community. Not in the sense of just accepting something because someone told you, but rather: Yes! This is really important! What does it mean to my life, to our life? There is a truth there that we will know by talking, by sharing. I really believe strongly that the Spirit is there working and moving among all of us. It's not that I accept it because someone else tells me, but we work it out together.

Theological Elements: Raymond's emphasis is on community. The church is the Spirit present and active among us as believers questioning and sharing. Truth is present, but can only be arrived at and understood within the honest struggle of the community.

---

[4]   From the *Theological Elements* document of *Session 3:*

Joseph's image occasioned some questioning from Raymond: "Isn't this really Reginald Bibby's cafeteria-type church membership that he describes in *Fragmented Gods* or *Mosaic Madness*: the consumer approach to religion—pick and choose what attracts you, etc.?"

At this point I intervened. I felt that Joseph's question and image is more than that. It is hermeneutical and touches the central fact that faith must be owned and personalized. "The child must grow up and leave the parent." This is creative. And living that faith means relativizing; that is, treating as non-important or even seeing as obstacle many of yesteryear's things of the faith and things still proposed today at times by the institutional church; e.g., clergy on a pedestal. Joseph was in agreement with my interpretation.

In this chapter, I have looked at Catholic teachers looking at themselves as Catholic teachers: what it means personally to be Roman Catholic today; what enriches them; what frustrates them. I believe that such a reflection is absolutely critical for any formation experience. Teachers in the Catholic school are expected to invite their students to follow Jesus as members of the Roman Catholic Christian community. Thus, it is essential that Catholic teachers have a strong sense of the church and their place in the church.

I prefer the vocabulary "sense of the church" to "knowledge of the church." For me, *sense* conveys more one's understanding of the church and one's position, commitment and role in the church. *Knowledge* can be abstract. *Knowledge* is not always personally integrated. *Sense*, on the other hand, implies a certain personalizing ownership of the church and of the church's mission. One's sense of the church has to do with attitudes and structures that promote faith and give hope and meaning. One's sense of the church also has to do with those attitudes and structures that may frustrate one's faith development and be obstacles to evangelizing effectively in our Catholic schools.

The conversation shows that the teachers are very taken with the communitarian, empowering ideal of church. Authoritarian attitudes and structures hurt people and are very counterproductive for doing Catholic education today. The teachers are also people of the sacraments. Clerical shortcomings and institutional scandals do not chase them out of the church. What they like most about the church is the personal meaning, hope and faith-sustenance they derive from the liturgy and their personal participation in the sacraments. In spite of the periodic frustration and disappointment they may experience because of the human and institutional flaws of the church, the sense of the sacraments continues to be an anchor for this group of teachers.

Seasonally, these teachers (and Catholic education generally) seem to be situated in late winter or early spring. In authoritarianism, outdated structures, patriarchal attitudes, and unimaginative efforts at preaching and evangelizing, there is still much winter about. But there are definite signs of spring. I feel that these teachers sense spring in the commitment and dedication they see in one another, in different types of community that nourish them humanly and spiritually, and in the realization that major change will have to come if we are to effectively evangelize in our Catholic schools as we move toward the millennium.

VIII

Making Sense
of Mixed Signals:
The Importance
of Interpretation

"Interpretation has to be more than just: 'This is the way I interpret it. This is my opinion.' It has to be from the gospel perspective: what is going on here as far as the gospel is concerned? Nowadays it is from the perspective of the disadvantaged, the preferential option for the poor. You interpret reality from the point of view of the poor. This is something many of us don't do well. We give an opinion, but what is the gospel principle? This is a central criterion of interpretation: the gospel! Or, use Micah! How do I act justly in this situation? How do I love tenderly? How do I walk humbly with God?" (Raymond, religion teacher).

In this chapter, I consider two further elements that I have made central to this particular model of a formation experience. I should add that the two elements—*evangelization* and *interpretation*—are both part of my passion regarding Catholic education. The teachers reflected on *evangelization* in *Session 5* and *interpretation* in *Session 6*. For me as facilitator-recorder, both sessions were surprisingly rich and interesting. I say "surprisingly" because, while I have worked on *evangelization* before, I discovered new angles of perspective and different questions. As for *interpretation*, the entire discussion was new, and the data it generated I found to be most interesting and useful for my own ministry. My discussion here of these two sessions consists of only fragments of the teachers' reflection and sharing on *evangelization* and *interpretation*, but these fragments are, I believe, essential fragments. There are four fundamental questions that should be asked of the data from these two sessions:

- How does formation take place?
- What does evangelization in the Catholic high school look like?
- What does interpretation mean in the context of the Catholic high school?
- How can interpretation be considered a means of evangelization?

These are the questions that preoccupy me as I continue to report on the conversation taking place between the teachers, as they reflect on their own very practical experience as Catholic educators. To begin I offer some further comments on the structure of this formation experience. Then, I continue to explore the relationship between the teachers' reflections and experience and some of the foundations I developed in Part Two. I conclude the chapter with commentaries on three questions pertaining to the way we evangelize today in the Catholic school.

Some Further Comments
on the Formation Experience

*On the Functioning of the Group and Atmosphere
for the Sessions*

There is much to be said about the chemistry of the group. I am very fortunate, I believe, because this group worked: there was a fine chemistry at play among the participants as I note in my journal for *Session 5:*

> The group works. There is a genuine liking and respect for each person. In terms of personal investment, it is my sense that the experienced teachers are taking this experience more seriously. I sense it in their preparation: they really do work at the readings; they give some good thought to whatever the theme is. Perhaps it is their friendship with me—doing it for me; perhaps it is their interest—they really are interested and committed; perhaps it is the nature of the experience. Probably it is all of this that accounts for their "quality participation." The beginning teachers: they are good! My sense is that time is a huge factor for them. To give two hours is already something. Preparation, though, is not as thorough. I guess it is natural: they are beginning teachers. That's the criterion. The experienced teachers are committed: that's one of the criteria according to which they were invited to participate.

I feel that similar groups would work equally well, since the make-up of the group is weighted in favour of it working. By this I mean the presence of the committed teachers. Given the criteria for selecting these teachers , there will most likely be a high degree of sensitivity and respect among them. It is sensitivity and respect, I believe, that are the two fundamental qualities of the participants, and necessary to make such a group work.

There is, as well, the question of climate for the group experience. For *Session 5* on *evangelization*, the climate or context for the reflection was shaped largely by two critical events that had taken place in school: a) the tragic car accident and death of Tanya the week before, followed by the memorial prayer service at school; b) the session for Ontario Academic Credit students the Friday before with "F," a person with AIDS. These two events were the source of some very good, practical theological reflection on evangelization.

A further comment is in order concerning the climate factor of the group experience. The climate of the group session will be fashioned significantly by the setting and time. The first three sessions took place in the evening, in my living room. The time and locale proved to be beneficial in several ways: away from school; more informal and casual; less rushed; an important "time-distance" between the work day and the session; generally more relaxed. But in January, winter was upon us. The teachers did not want to go home after school and come back, so we decided to meet after school. In my journal for *Session 5* I commented on the problems with this arrangement:

> The beginning of the session is slow! Is it the new locale? Is it the time: right after school, towards the end of the semester when there is so much going on? Is it the fact that they have to stay tonight for Grade-Eight orientation? Is it the theme?

> Here again I come back to the *time* question. The whole enterprise has to do with forming teachers, but it does take time. It takes time to reflect, to read, to prepare, to make journal entries, etc. The school year, indeed each semester, has its own beat! Once you get going, so much is done according to deadlines: papers to mark; tests to make and mark; teams to coach; newspapers to put out; events to organize, etc. These folks are being good to me. But the time

thing really has to be considered in setting up any type of reflection experience.

On the Prayer Component of the Experience

According to the evaluations, the prayer component of the experience was highly valued. As facilitator, I considered this part of my service to the group. But at the same time, it was a key dimension of my facilitation to create the prayer around the theme, so that the Word of God could be heard by the teachers. While generally happy with the prayer, I did encounter difficulties. In the first place, it was the *time and place* again that proved to be problematic, as I recorded in my journal for *Session 6:*

> A note on prayer! I notice a difference in our prayer at 3:15 as opposed to prayer for the evening sessions. The evening seems to be more relaxed, and it is easier to enter into the prayer. The 3:15 starting time, while favoured by the group, is both hectic and fatiguing. It takes more time to get into the session. There is the hustle to get to the session and the fatigue at the end of the teaching day. Again, what this brings up is the question of *time and place* to do this type of formation.

A second source of difficulty for prayer was my own zeal and personal penchant to expect too much, and consequently, to do too much. This is best evidenced in the analysis of the prayer I recorded in my journal for *Session 5:*

> I put together a very rich, content-heavy prayer. I "theologized" the prayer, using passages from G.&S. (*Gaudium et Spes*) and E.N. (*Evangelii Nuntiandi*) and *This Moment of Promise* and Luke 4:16. The passages I chose had to do with the theology of evangelization. My idea was to include some theology in the prayer. Each person read a passage. There was Taize background music and time between readings. My hunch is that I tried to do too much. I was disap-

pointed that in the reflection more references were not made to some of the texts, to that theology. I was disappointed, too, that Paul VI's "upsetting quality of evangelization" did not come out more. There really was not enough time. Perhaps a more didactic session is needed every now and then to present some of that theology.

In general, prayer seemed to be most appreciated when it was simple: quiet time, some meditative music, a passage from the Scriptures that shed light and meaning on the reflection.

An Observation on Evaluation

In the next chapter, I evaluate the over-all experience. Here I offer but a brief preliminary observation on the importance of evaluation for the formation experience. I direct this observation, in particular, to the need for evaluation for each session. From journal entry for *Session 6:*

> A word about evaluation! At the suggestion of Gregory, we stopped a bit early and took 5-10 minutes and wrote an initial evaluation. I asked them, as well, to do the evaluation drawn up for this session. In asking for the return of the evaluations I don't want to nag. I ask tactfully and persistently, but I get only 1/2 to 3/4 of them per session. Again, it is the experienced group that is more faithful. But I do see how important some kind of evaluation is for such sessions. The evaluation is important and necessary as an adult education tool. It makes for more complete learning, to have to think and own what you just did.

Continuing the Report
on the Catholic Teachers' Faith Journey

The Reflection on Evangelization

The background readings for this session were essentially passages selected from *On Evangelization in the Modern World*, which I considered as a theoretical foundation in Chapter 2. The reflection questions were designed to invite the teachers to review their own evangelizing experience in the Catholic high school. The questions also asked the teachers to give concrete examples. Generally, both the beginning and experienced teachers understand evangelization as having very much to do with the Catholic character of the school. They would describe it as living gospel values and inviting the students to do the same. I highlight three aspects of the sharing which I believe describe well the challenge of evangelizing in the Catholic high school and the formation needed to meet this challenge.

1.   Evangelization and the Power of the Personal Story

Joseph emphasized the power of personal story as being the most personal and effective way of communicating one's own faith convictions and values:

> The more we share of our story! We all have a story to tell. We talked earlier about this. Sharing your story with kids or sharing your vulnerability with them or sharing when you screwed up yourself. I think this does them a lot of good. I always have the idea that my point is received—for example, talking about self-respect—when I can personalize it, using examples from my own life.

And Gregory relates the impact "F's" story had on the 175 Ontario Academic Credit students:

> We had a superb session for the OACs last Friday: a reflection on AIDS. A nurse talked about transmission, statistics,

ways to protect yourself, responsibility. And then there was a person with AIDS. He told his story from his youth. The 175 kids were mesmerized! He was abused as a youth, hit the streets, drugs, prostitution. He met a girl. She refused to have intercourse with him until they were married. He turned to faith and the spiritual life. He dedicates his life to telling his story. His story impacted on those kids. That was evangelizing. He spoke about Jesus, but not in a TV way.

Not only is personal story an effective way of evangelizing students, but in the group formation experience itself, *story* proved to be an excellent means of sharing experience and giving life, colour and detail to particular strategies. Ann was a very adept story-teller throughout the sessions, having a wonderfully reflective insight into her own experience, always commanding the attention of the group, and able to make substantial points through her story:

Evangelization has to be real! In a sense you can't plan to evangelize. You react. There was one situation with a Grade-Eleven class a couple of years ago. In my class that day I had three exceptional students [students who are educationally handicapped] and four behavioural problems—one in particular who had been suspended and so on. I had a film set up with questions. And then a student came to the door and wanted to talk to me. It was critical: something about suicide! I went outside the room talking to her, persuading her to go for counselling. I was sitting on the stairs with her when one of the special education kids came running violently out of the door, screaming and crying, telling me that the other kids had been throwing chalk at her and swearing. A real explosion! She sort of tackled me, arms around my neck, saying: "Don't make me go back!" She was in tears. The other girl was sitting beside me. So I asked the suicide girl to go down to talk to the vice-principal. I had her promise me. She promised. And then I had to go into the class. I was very upset and angry.

I went into the class, tears coming down my face. The room was absolutely quiet, nobody saying a word. Now I don't know why I did this—that's why I say that you have to react in the right way; I said to the kids to get out paper and pencil, and each one write to me and tell me what happened in this room. I was amazed at the reaction. They did what I asked. I got all those papers and eventually a name; so many of them wanted to do something and were ashamed that they hadn't done it. The upshot was: this particular student came back and apologized to the whole class and to the student individually. I think they learned more from this than anything I taught all semester. But I couldn't plan any of that. But my anger was real: it has to be a real reaction.

In my journal for *Session 5* I made the following observation of Ann's story:

Ann's story to the group really is a moment of ministry or an evangelizing moment—through story! As she talks, Marisa, Marie and Arthur are nodding agreement at different times. Everyone is very focused on her. [It] demonstrates clearly the power of personal story.

2.   Evangelization and the Teachable Moment

I have already made note of the two special influences shaping the session on evangelization: Tanya's death and funeral, and "F", the person with AIDS. Both of these influences underscored the potential of *the teachable moment* for evangelization. Teachable moments are moments that are extraordinary. They are moments that offer a genuine opportunity for reflecting on purpose and meaning in life, or what Thomas Groome terms *the ultimacy questions*. Tanya's death and its impact on the students proved to be data for a profound reflection on experience. The experienced teachers were more comfortable with this kind of experience, and more able to process with some ease:

> Ann: I had a Grade-Nine student commenting on Tanya's memorial service. What really struck this girl was the number of teachers who were crying. It really touched her that we could be touched by this. The kids don't often see this because we have to be in control. And we need to be, in order to carry out our job. This was extraordinary for her.

> Donna: I had a girl tell me in guidance that she didn't want to die, . . . but felt a lot better that, if she did die, she would get something like the prayer we had for Tanya. And another kid in Grade Ten came in and said to me: she needs to rethink how she acts. She was so touched by the kids who spoke about Tanya. She said: "Wonder if something happened to me, and kids couldn't say anything about me." And she didn't know Tanya.

> Ann: I had a lot of Grade-Eleven kids who were in some of the classes with her. They started to talk about: "Well, is there something after this life?" They went into resurrection. One girl kind of thought it was like the Easter Bunny or Santa Claus. Now she is really rethinking its meaning.

> Donna: I couldn't get over as the kids were going out: how they touched Tanya's father! What a remarkable thing. Not being able to say much, they sensed how important feeling was—the touch—to reassure the father.

Joseph commented in his usual thoughtful way on the meaning of the teachable moment itself, and the need for awareness and sensitivity on the part of the teacher-evangelizer:

> I think those teachable moments come along. We usually talk about them in terms of curriculum. But I think that they are even more present in life; for example, treating people with respect. The teachable moment is always when the kid

is most vulnerable. When he is hurting the most, or when she is screwed up so much. They are at a point in their lives where anything you do is magnified in importance. The lesson really comes across.

3.   *On Evangelizing the Evangelizers*

Several experienced teachers remarked on the importance of ongoing reflection and sharing if the teacher evangelizers are to be evangelized themselves. While Mario and Michael did not disagree, they insisted something like this is not easy to do on your own, and a concrete, practical aid is needed:

> Mario: It is hard to do it on your own. Someone has to stimulate that reflection or force you into it. And you need the time!

> Michael: In some of the P.D. [professional development] days we have, what I hear a lot is "evangelizing the evangelizers," but where are the concrete, practical curriculum aids and techniques? We need techniques!

Donna, however, suspicious of recipes and "how-to" packages, continued to promote the type of reflection on experience that is at the very heart of this formation experience:

> This kind of dialogue or reflection is really good because it triggers things in you and helps you remember! And I don't know about a "how-to" book. It's better to talk and share stories and experiences.

In *On Evangelization in the Modern World*, Paul VI speaks of witnessing in an authentic way to the Christian life as the first means of evangelization:

> Modern men and women listen more willingly to witnesses than to teachers, and if they do listen to teachers, it is because they are witnesses (*E.N.*, 41).

In the Catholic high school, teachers must keep learning this lesson. Because Catholic educators are teachers, the temptation is to content oneself with teaching the Good News and simply assume that the witnessing is there. But much more than that is needed, as Paul VI warns, if the teaching is to take root. Sharing one's personal story, especially through actions, gestures and example, and seizing on the teachable moments both life and curriculum offer—all of this is very consistent with Paul VI's theology of evangelization. And how does one teach this to beginning teachers? How does one form teachers to evangelize in this fashion? I believe Donna is right. There are no "how-to" books. Coming together in faith and good will to reflect on what it means to teach in a Catholic school—to reflect on the vocation of the Catholic educator—to share personal successes and failures in evangelizing: this is a most effective way of evangelizing the evangelizers. But I think Mario is right also: "Someone has to stimulate that reflection or force you into it. . . . [A]nd you need the time."

The disappointing note in this reflection on evangelization in the Catholic high school is not anything that was shared, but rather, what was *not* shared. There was very little emphasis given to Paul VI's "upsetting notion of evangelization" (*E.N.*, 18 and 19). In analyzing this, I am not sure how to explain it. Perhaps there was not time enough in the session. Perhaps the influences of Tanya and "F" took the reflection in a different direction. Or, perhaps there was not sufficient ownership of this critical principle of Paul VI's theology of evangelization. Quite possibly the answer is wrapped up in all three possibilities. The *upsetting* dimension was touched on, but only at the end of the session. In the session on interpretation, however, there was more of an emphasis on this critical principle.

The Reflection on Interpretation

In the reflections on experience thus far, the idea of the need to interpret has surfaced consistently. In education, in our social, economic and political structures, there is much ambiguity, confusion and uncertainty afoot. The absolute responses of yesteryear have all but disappeared. As for the church and the things of faith, many Catholic educators admit confusion and insecurity: how to discern; how to read the signs of the times; how to select what is appropriate and adequate; how to make sense out of the mixed signals emanating from our social and church context. This description and these questions, I believe, are a fair reflection of some of the sentiments and concerns of more than a few Catholic educators across the province.[1]

As background reading for this session on interpretation I created "Ten Examples on the Need to Interpret." These are verbatim quotes of various teacher-participants recorded during the first five sessions; they recount stories and examples touching on the need to interpret. To begin the actual session I proposed two concrete situations calling for interpretation— examples from recent news reports. I described this introduction in my journal for *Session 6:*

> In a preamble or introduction—the first time I give such a long introduction—I focus this session on the teachers' own need to interpret and the need for time to help students inter- pret and learn the skills and spirit of interpretation. To frame the question more concretely, I refer to two articles that appeared in the last couple of days: *Toronto Star*, February 1, 1992, religion page: "Catholic newspaper sparks contro-

---

[1]   Refer to Chapter 3: "Cultural Foundations," footnote 39, which, through anecdote, provides two examples of Catholic educators struggling with the question of interpretation. I offered these same examples to the teacher-par- ticipants as background reading to prepare for this session on interpretation.

versy by refusing ad for book." The reference is to the *Catholic Register's* refusal to print an ad for *In the Eye of the Catholic Storm* by Mary Jo Leddy, Doug Roche and Bishop Remi DeRoo. I also read from *Catholic New Times*, February 2, 1992: "Tensions heighten over monk's speaking tour." There is a challenging quote here from Walter Principe[2] applicable to teachers in Catholic schools and the tensions they experience, tensions I feel to be the stuff of interpretation. There are good quotes from Leddy, Roche, DeRoo and Principe.

The data from *Session 6* is a useful resource for different understandings of what it is to interpret and how Catholic educators can go about interpreting. I present but a sample of some very rich insights.

Question: What are the ingredients of interpretation, the skill, the spirit and attitude of interpretation, for the Catholic educator?

Raymond: Interpretation has to be more than just, "This is the way I interpret it. This is my opinion." It has to be from the gospel perspective: what is going on here as far as the gospel is concerned? Nowadays it is from the perspective of the disadvantaged, the preferential option for the poor. You

---

[2]   *Catholic New Times* (February 2, 1992), p. 12. Father Walter Principe noted that some Catholics

> . . . are confused when some bishops and priests lump all Catholic teaching together as if everything they teach is infallible and unchangeable; [these] Catholics [are] disheartened when discussion of non-infallible and changing issues is closed off.

Commenting on the "tension" felt by many (he mentioned especially teachers in Catholic schools), Principe acknowledged that not all such tension is a bad thing.

> Catholic teaching should put us under some pressure not to conform to the culture. But sometimes [clergy] can get caught inside a closed circle and can stop listening to the problems people have with what they are teaching.

the disadvantaged, the preferential option for the poor. You interpret reality from the point of view of the poor. This is something many of us don't do well. We give an opinion, but what is the gospel principle? This is a central criterion of interpretation: the gospel! Or use Micah! How do I act justly in this situation? How do I love tenderly? How do I walk humbly with God?

Ann: One of the ingredients of interpretation is to take the Word. Go directly to the gospel. And there are a lot of questions in helping people interpret. You ask: what do you think it is to act justly in this situation?

Joseph: Interpreting is something like conscience. You have to inform your conscience, so we have to study. We have to go to the authority. But to keep in mind now that one authority does not an answer make. There are different situations. Look also at the different theological and church views on things. For example, those articles! [from the *Toronto Star* and *Catholic New Times*]. But you can't just use your own opinion on a thing. To interpret you have to inform yourself about the gospel. We talked earlier: evangelizers must evangelize themselves. That's a part of it. We have to ask: what does the church say? Is there controversy? What are the views? But this is not to sit and pick and choose. It's a struggle that involves study and prayer.

Question: How do we help students interpret?

Joseph: Kids in Grade Nine are in the process of leaving childhood faith. And they will soon get away from: "Tell me what is right and wrong." They'll get into that gray area. That means we have to interpret. That's part of owning our faith: asking questions.

Michael: I have a difficult time understanding what you really mean for kids to interpret as they are growing and developing. Is it moral development we're talking about? Interpreting what? The teachings of Jesus?

Raymond: We need to work from the kids' experience and help them question, help them interpret. You can't tell them!

Joseph: I agree you can't tell them, but if they ask you what you think, you have to explain to them where you are at; share your struggle and story. They have to go through the struggle, the process of learning to interpret. We can't do it for them.

I analyzed this exchange among Joseph, Michael and Raymond in my journal for *Session 6:*

The experienced teachers clearly work out of their experience. The beginning teachers just don't have the same quality or length of experience. I notice how the experienced teachers elaborate on moral development: for the Grade-Nines it's black and white; for the seniors it's more gray: lots of questions. Adult faith is ownership and implies a lot of interpretation to take place in the ownership of faith.

Joseph gives good, concrete examples of the stuff of interpretation to Mario and Michael. For example: pre-marital living together as apprenticeship vs. the teaching of the church; ripping off a tee-shirt and bullying and the need to reflect this behaviour back to the students so that they can review it in light of the gospel. The point is that as teachers we need to question the kids so that they will question: What is right? What is wrong? There is a good dialogue: Mario looks for the possibilities. How often do I see someone bully or rip off something? Joseph says it's a conscious sort of thing; bring it up hypothetically in class: "I came across this! What do you think?" Mario agrees; he sees. And then Joseph uses examples from guidance: concrete examples on how to intervene, how to challenge the kids. And Michael and Donna enter the exchange. Joseph says: "We have to call the kids to look at their behaviour!"

Michael makes the observation that much of this process is built on experience, but beginning teachers don't have that much teaching experience! Along with this he asks for more structure, facilitation, a brief teaching-input component for each session on the part of the facilitator.

This is a good and important question: one I had not really considered. Obviously a process based on experience leaves the beginning teacher with a restricted experience base. Another factor related to this is the *reflection factor*. The reflection quotient—whether or not you are given easily to reflecting, whether you have the skills, the disposition, also touches on beginning teachers. I exempt the experienced teachers here because one of the criteria in choosing them was their reflective dispositions. I would go further and say that "experience" the way I use it in this project contains within it that reflective capacity.

During the course of the reflection, the teachers were asked to suggest ingredients that go into interpreting. I recorded their suggestions.

Ingredients of Interpretation

- It is best done with others in community.

- It is more than just my opinion; it is from the gospel view.

- Use Micah: how do I act justly? love tenderly? walk humbly with God?

- Questions must be involved; it is a struggle.

- Serious prayer and reflection on a decision or problem; trust in the dynamic presence of the Holy Spirit.

- Refer to Catholic teachings.

- Have a good understanding of what reality is.

- Vatican II recognizes and understands the world and its "dramatic characteristics"; (this was the group's code word for society's "screwed-upness").

- You can't lose hope, can't be fatalistic; hope is life-giving.

- It is like informing your conscience; the steps: prayer, the gospel, church teaching, seeking out authority and authorities.

Interpretation, Conversation and the Catholic School Community

In Chapter 3, I commented on David Tracy's notion of *interpretation*. Inherent in Tracy's understanding of *interpretation* are resistance and hope: a *resistance* to the powers and ideologies of our time and place, and *hope,* which is both confidence in God's continued action in the world and a patient waiting for the goodness that could be. *Resistance* for the Catholic educator means first and foremost to be aware of and ready to interpret the plurality and ambiguity that so characterize our present social and ecclesial context. In addition, to resist involves working out a personal approach to interpret, to decide, to select a course of action or behaviour that adequately meets the demands of a particular situation or question. *Hope*, for the Catholic educator, is the enduring confidence that the Holy Spirit is present in it all; that the ideals of renewal conceived in Vatican II can still be realized; and that ultimately, in spite of the urgency of the crisis, it really is God's problem. I believe the preceding discussion of the teachers' understanding and use of interpretation is clear evidence that there are some remarkable personal approaches about, personal methods that are both responsible and respectful of the individual's personal ownership of faith and membership in the community of believers, the church.

David Tracy proposes conversation as the process for arriving at a relatively adequate understanding of truth. In his oral evaluation for *Session 6,* Raymond, in insisting on the community context for interpreting, resonates with David Tracy's notion of conversation:

> Raymond: I think interpretation is of central importance. I know that adult contact with young people is the primary thing in the evangelization of adolescents. So if that is what it is, then we need to know what we are about. Reflecting in a small group: it's like struggling together. We say: "I'm not sure about this!" We talk it out with other people of faith. If it is left to your own individual thing, it's not right. Interpretation has to do with the faith community . . ., and how do I know that, unless I sit down and talk with you. Interaction and dialogue help clarify where I stand and why we are doing this. And on some of the issues . . . my opinion may be very different, but then I understand you more, and that in turn will alter my opinion.

In my journal for *Session 6,* I made this comment on Raymond's contribution:

> In the evaluation, Raymond made mention of the community—conversation dimension of interpretation. This made me think of David Tracy's *conversation idea* as the way of working towards truth in a context of plurality and ambiguity. We need to dialogue and listen, and that's how we grow and change. I alter my understanding of truth by running into and engaging in your understanding of truth.

Interpretation: A Dimension of Evangelization

Interpretation can be understood as an element of evangelization in two ways. The process of interpreting can be understood as an evangelizing experience for the Catholic educator. As we have seen in reviewing the ingredients for interpretation of the teacher-participants: personal reflection, prayer and questioning are all essential to the process. In other words, the empowering and enabling presence of the Spirit is understood. It is understood, as well, that for Catholic educators the community context for interpreting is vital. Thus, the process itself can become an experience of evangelization. In interpreting—in working through the process—in the struggle to discern what is the gospel way: how to act justly, love tenderly and walk humbly with God in this particular situation, one is evangelized. The mutuality of evangelization comes into play when one struggles to interpret in community. Interpretation in this sense can be understood as the attempt to own and personalize faith, and that, it seems to me, is evangelization. It is, as well, ongoing formation!

Introducing young people to the spirit and skills of interpretation is a second way that interpretation can be understood as an element of evangelization. To accompany students, to help them understand the struggle that is part and parcel of living the gospel in an adult way, to assist them in their interpretation of the ultimacy questions in life—all of this can be evangelizing activity. To be sure, the dynamic presence of the Holy Spirit is understood in such activity. Joseph is eloquent in his explanation of how interpretation is a method of evangelizing:

> I think interpretation is something we can always do. Whenever things go on—to take our mission, our vocation as evangelizers seriously: sometimes kids turn us right off if we preach at them. But situations arise that are difficult for kids to interpret. I really do think that most kids search for meaning in some way. They look for reasons. I believe that if we interpret things in a gospel . . . Catholic way . . . I think that this is really important. Tanya's death was a terrible tragedy, but the positive things—the way we tried to put that

in perspective and interpret it—I really do think that this is an important thing for us as evangelizers.

Commentary

On Accompanying the Adolescent

Throughout the course of the sessions on evangelization and interpretation, there were varied and valuable insights into the personality and habits of the adolescent. This knowledge, too, is of critical importance for any formation experience of teachers in the Catholic high school. For the Catholic educator there is a need to know adolescents and to adapt evangelization to their needs and their context. Paul VI insists on this evangelizing strategy:

> Evangelization loses much of its force and effectiveness if it does not take into consideration the actual people to whom it is addressed—their language, signs, symbols, questions and concrete life situation (*E.N.* 63).

For these teachers, awareness of adolescents and their needs and questions was very much a given. I noted in my journal for *Session 5:*

> There were some very valuable insights on the part of the teachers as to what makes the adolescent tick. Good commentary on the psychology of the adolescent: their vulnerability; afraid to take baseball caps off at liturgy because their hair is not in place; inadequacies and jealousies and insecurities; the influence and pressure of peers, etc.

Michael and Raymond concur that as evangelizers they need both a good understanding of the adolescent reality and the insights and patience to walk with them.

Michael: And you better have a good understanding of what reality is today if you are going to interpret! This is really important: to know the kids; to know where they are coming from.

Raymond: In the reading, DeRoo said something about journey and pilgrimage, and that's, I believe, what faith is. As teachers we need to journey with the young; to go to where they are—their experiences. Now, that's a different perception than saying: "Here, kid: this is the package; this is what it is!" But when you journey with someone, that challenges your own perspective! Things aren't written in stone. If they were, that really takes out the action of the Spirit. That for me is interpreting. You can't just dictate and say this is the way it is!

Interpretation and Controversy

Since the social and ecclesial context is so marked by plurality and ambiguity, there are bound to be moments of controversy. This is the built-in tension to interpreting. In the classroom and in the larger context of interpreting just what it is to be Catholic today, there are the inevitable tensions and controversies. Ann underlined the necessity of being cautious when dealing with certain issues:

It is more difficult with controversial issues. Kids will go home and say to their parents: "The teacher said this about contraception or birth control." And some of these parents are very conservative. When I teach my parenting course and we get into that, I know I have to be very careful the way I say things.

In view of that example and several others like it, I made the following note in my journal for *Session 6:*

The radical conservative element in the church is a factor in the classroom. In my experience these folks are not that numerous, but somehow they manage to serve as watchdogs, especially regarding family life education, to which they are opposed. This fact certainly contributes to the atmosphere of the context in which we do our interpreting. It is part of the tension.

In the oral evaluation following the interpretation session, Donna raised the hypothetical question of the teacher who is in conflict with church teaching. This is one of the few times I left my perch as observer and became a participant. I explained this in the following entry in my journal for *Session 6:*

> Donna's question in the evaluation was a real surprise: "What happens if a teacher has a real conflicting view with the church?" The question was directed at me, and given the fact that Michael, just a minute before, had asked for more facilitation (in an input sort of way), I tried to respond. My response brought in Ann, Donna and Raymond and enabled the group to look at another aspect of interpretation yet untouched: the hierarchy of questions or values—e.g., abortion vs. birth control—and the need for the teacher to assess appropriate value or weight or importance to an issue. Raymond was very helpful in pointing out how *formation* (background) and *interpretation* are mutually related and important.

> Donna: What happens if a teacher has a conflicting view with the church?

> Facilitator-Recorder: A very good question. For example, there could be a person in good faith who sees nothing wrong with abortion. For me, in this case, my principle is that given the fact that the teaching of the church is so clear on abortion, you must be quiet. You can't express your own

views on that, and even if pressed, you should find a way of not answering. The Catholic high school is a public institution, with intimate faith ties to the teaching of the Roman Catholic Church. To work in the Catholic high school is to acknowledge and respect these realities. If it is too much a question of conscience, then I feel the person should not be a teacher in the Catholic high school.

Ann: But that's interpretation itself as to which issues!

Facilitator-Recorder: Exactly! Which issues? Some ethical questions are more serious than others. But already here you make judgements. You are interpreting.

Ann: Yes! You have to make those judgements.

Donna: Okay, that's you as a Catholic teacher! But not everyone on staff is a Catholic teacher. That's another dilemma.

Facilitator-Recorder: Yes. But in a sense I feel it might even be easier because they can suspend their opinion. They can say: "Okay, we're here in a Catholic high school. We have to do it according to the Catholic framework." But I believe it is more difficult in a way for us being Catholics and disagreeing. But all of this is a whole other discussion—a long one at that.

Raymond: But I think that that's why the two of them have to go together: the forming thing and interpretation! I think interpretation is of central importance, but we need understanding.

Conservatives, Liberals and Catholic Education

I conclude this chapter on interpretation as a method of evangelization with a personal, interpretive observation. In terms of church politics, are the teachers conservatives or liberals? Are they on the right or the left? Or, are they in between? The liberal-conservative references came up several times: when considering controversial issues; in the discussion on whether or not to print the ad for the book in the Catholic paper; while reflecting on women's issues. I refer once more to my journal for *Session 6*. I believe the interpretation of the teachers rendered there is accurate and could apply generally to Catholic educators across Canada:

> Time and again in the discussions, there surfaced different notions or ways of being Catholic. There are the radical conservatives and conservatives. It is important to recognize this since it is our context and contributes to the tension and complexity in interpreting. It is interesting to note that most of the group can identify conservative or right-wing modes of behaviour and positions and even publications. Yet, with but two or three exceptions, they are really not familiar with *Catholic New Times*, which would be considered on the left. Nor are they aware of radical liberals. I would say that the teachers, by osmosis, live Catholicism in a Vatican II renewed way. They recognize the need for changes. They would be supportive of democratizing trends in the church. The group's left-wing or liberal bias [in the eyes of the right] would be seen in their support of equality for women in the church, including ordination; they would follow the Canadian Bishops' commentary on *Humanae Vitae*; and the need to de-clericalize the church and empower the laity while emphasizing community. Most of this, it seems to me, is pretty mainstream English Canadian Roman Catholic thinking since Vatican II. Implied, too, is the strong conviction that truth is not the preserve of any one caste in the church—liberal or conservative: that the Holy Spirit is gift to the entire community of believers.

The Potential
for This Model

"Any problem is best tackled by brainstorming with peers. Our questions were not lunchroom-type topics or discussions, but they were questions that should definitely be addressed. The most valuable thing for me? It was a joint effort between new and more experienced teachers, sharing their views on Catholic education. I feel that such sharing is really important to understand students today. During our sessions I was also taking the OECTA Religion Course, Part One. I feel the OECTA course was somewhat weak in applying 'Catholicity' concretely to our everyday situations. As Catholic teachers, we need to share more and more to meet the demands of the situations we must face" (Marisa, science teacher).

"I would endorse this model. It certainly was a growth experience for me, maybe even more than for the new teachers because I could go back in mind and remember situations and events where strategies worked or didn't. I could relate to what another person was feeling or experiencing. The young members had so much to offer—a freshness in their outlook, honesty, enthusiasm, a need for change—this I

found to be renewing. 'Renewal' is a good word—that's what this model does for experienced teachers. I often felt like a thief because I felt I should be giving more. For sure I was taking a lot from this group" (Donna, business teacher).

What possibilities does this model of formation have for teachers in Catholic schools? What is its potential? How does one evaluate it? What implications could this model of formation have for publicly funded Catholic schools? These are the questions I pursue in this concluding chapter. Reflection sessions on formation and on the evaluation of the group experience generate the content for the chapter. I report and comment on the conversations of these sessions under four headings:

- Teachers reflect on formation;

- Teachers reflect on this model of formation;

- The findings of a reflective practitioner;

- The implications and challenges deriving from this formation experience.

Teachers Reflect on Formation

The notion of formation itself was the focus for *Session 7*. As preparation for this session, the teachers were asked to give some thought to teacher training generally, and more particularly, to the way teachers are prepared to teach in a *Catholic* school. The reflection questions were designed to have the teachers review their own particular training experiences, both professional training at a faculty of education and theological training at a faculty or elsewhere. Included in the set of questions was one that was more autobiographical and reflective in nature: *Can you pinpoint and elaborate on two or three key moments in your own development as a person?*

Autobiographical Reflections

The teachers found the autobiographical reflection to be on the difficult side, although it yielded some very rich sharing regarding the way faith, values and personal convictions have been shaped. It was clear that strong personal witness and familial/communal witness had a crucial impact on the faith development of some of the teachers. I believe, too, that this same type of witness was instrumental in shaping the way they act and behave as Catholic teachers, that is, the way they understand and live out their vocation as Catholic educators. In my journal for *Session 7*, I pose two questions touching on formation, both of which follow from the autobiographical sharing:

• With so much importance and value given to family for the generation of faith, values and morals—even if some of this is a cultural thing—what does this mean for today, when many teachers coming into the Catholic system do not have such a background? And what does this mean down the road for the Catholic character of our schools?

• People were clearly interested and attentively listening during the story-telling part of our session. What does this say about story-telling as a means of formation and the sharing of faith?

On the Participation of the Beginning Teachers

As we approached the end of the experience, it was more and more evident that the participants were comfortable with one another. In my journal I wrote:

A comment is in order on the development of the group as group! On a few occasions today—I think of Marisa and Marie—people mentioned how comfortable they were in the group. Such words as "non-threatening," "trusting," "open," "a very comfortable group in comparison to other experiences" came up. It was remarked, too, that at the beginning it was somewhat difficult for some because they didn't know the others that well, and they were not sure. Now they feel very comfortable. I think that these comments say a lot about the quality of the people who participate in the group.

On the formation theme in particular the beginning teachers were very animated and contributed more often than the experienced teachers. I believe the formation question—especially *initial* formation—really struck a chord with the beginning teachers. The discussion focused on their immediate needs and concerns, and they could refer easily to their own faculty of education experience, which is still fresh in mind if not in practice. For the experienced teachers, on the other hand, teacher training was in the distant past. Their immediate educational needs and questions were not quite as acute as those of the beginning teachers.

A Different Strategy

For each session I generally let the discussion unfold and take its own course. I was facilitator, but I was also a recorder. I intervened only to keep the group on topic or to move the group to a consideration of the next question. In this session on *formation*, however, I pointedly suggested that for two questions the group go clockwise in their sharing. I explained this strategy in my journal:

> There is a strategy I employed in this session that probably comes from reflecting on the last session and [remembering] how quiet the beginning teachers seemed to be. For questions 1 and 3 I invited the group to go around the circle and share. This technique certainly worked. I think the autobiographical nature of these questions had something to do with that. Perhaps, in the final recommendation of the model it would be wise to build a question appropriate for this

strategy into each reflection session. From the beginning, at least once each session, go around the circle asking each person to share. But be sure to keep it non-threatening.

On Training to Teach ... and On Training to Teach in a Catholic School

In my journal for *Session 7*, I recorded the following reflections on teacher training and training to teach in a Catholic school. In terms of critique or evaluation, these are comments and opinions of the teachers in the group and are reflective only of their experience. They are, however, interesting and revealing.

1. For the experienced teachers it was trial by fire! There was not too much positive to say about their formation. Very little or no practice-teaching. Social life was good! No input re: a Catholic school system or formation for Catholic education.

2. For beginning teachers there was a poor experience of the religion course at the college of education: mainly lectures and hand-outs; too theoretical and not hands-on or practical enough.

3. There was a good assessment of the strengths and weaknesses of the Ontario English Catholic Teachers' Association (OECTA) Religion Course, Part One (through the year and in summer):

Weaknesses

- too lecture-oriented
- too theoretical
- disconnected
- not relevant; unfocused
- poorly organized

Strengths

- mixture of input and personal sharing
- practical aspects of preparing prayer and liturgy
- sense of community
- reflection on experience

N.B.: Generally the summer course was found to be much richer than the year-long evening course.

4. In teacher formation (training), monitoring, evaluating and regular feedback were considered to be very important.

5. It was unanimous that in any formation experience there has to be structure, focus and organization.

6. It was pointed out that we learn a lot re: techniques, classroom management strategies and tricks of the trade from other teachers. It was strongly felt that this model we are developing would be very useful for Catholic teacher formation.

Commentary

Which comes first: the theory or the practice? This is a question I have worked away at, off and on, for most of my years in ministry. I have long been convinced, for example, of the primacy of a solid theological background for ministry. Initially, my "solid theological background" had largely to do with an academic-style theology: systematics, ethics, scripture, and so forth. More recently I have become increasingly open to a practical theology: a theology born of a personal or group reflection in faith on the meaning of a practice or experience or life-situation. In the actual reflection on the doing of an action—as in an apostolate or ministry—a theology is generated. The theory becomes clear in the praxis. To apply my question, then, to formation for Catholic teachers: which should come first—an adequate theological background or a reflective practice? In my journal for *Session 7* I continued to work at this question:

> Mario's critique of the religion course at the college of education is interesting. He says: "Too many lectures and not enough practical experience."

> Mario: At the university, the college of education, the religion or theology course was not appropriate. Kind of useless. Basically it was historical; a lecture-type class; handouts; nothing about Catholic teachers and teaching. I didn't get much out of it; just put my time in. No reflections. Maybe it was partly my fault because I turned it off, but I really didn't get anything from the lectures. It was a bad experience. But the summer Part One course was totally different. I got a lot from that. Regarding teacher formation: the most useful part for me was the practice teaching. Not enough of it. Generally: too much theory and not enough practice.

It had long been my view that teachers need that theory, that understanding, that background before they practice. Perhaps my approach was the wrong approach. Perhaps we will come to see and understand theory and theology—and the importance of theory and theology—in the doing of it: in the action and the experience. Perhaps the preliminary need is to equip student-teachers with just enough basic "how-to's" and skills—survival strategies—to get into the action and experience. Then, through reflection on that action and experience, the what, the why and the where of the theory and theology—their necessity and importance—will become apparent. In a way, in this model we tried to do that. We got at the "understanding" through reflection on our actions and experience; the reflection on interpretation was a good example of this.

Teachers Reflect on *This* Model of Formation

Throughout this book I have stressed why some unique *formation* is an imperative for teachers in Catholic high schools. My notion of formation is clear: formation is invitational, not mandatory; it is both initial and ongoing; it is more than training or skills development in that it intends to touch a person's spirit. It should attend to the vocation dimension of teaching in the Catholic school. Formation privileges in a special way both the experience and the life-situation of the one being formed. And finally, there is an adult-learning mutuality to formation when Catholic educators form one another.

I have also proposed one particular *model* of formation that could readily be adapted in most if not all Catholic schools. In Part Three, I have been describing this model and analyzing one experience of it. Within that experience, each of the proposed constitutive elements of formation is operative. My intention now is to report on the teachers' evaluation of this model of formation—the eight-month-long conversation between beginning and experienced teachers on the vocation of teaching in a Catholic school.

Evaluation of the Experience

Throughout the eight sessions, there were three key moments for evaluation: an oral evaluation *at the end* of each session, a written evaluation *after* each session, and the eighth session itself—an evaluation of the entire experience that included a detailed, 15-page written assessment of the total experience. In this discussion on evaluation I draw from the data found in these evaluations.

The evaluation of each session focused on four critical elements of the process: the quantity and relevance of the readings; the learning outcomes for the sessions; the quality of group life; and an appreciation of the prayer component. The *oral* evaluation would take place in the last ten minutes of the session. This was an opportunity for each teacher to share reactions or feelings about the session. Teachers were invited to share on one or another of the elements listed above. The *written* evaluation, a two-page form eliciting feedback, was distributed at the end of the session. Teachers were asked to return it to me before the following session. These forms were unsigned. I received, on the average, about 60% of them over the eight sessions. As a general recapitulation, I present a synthesis of the teacher-participants' evaluation of the formation experience drawing on data from both the oral and written evaluations.

On the Quantity and Relevance of the Background Reading

The evaluations of the background readings were generally positive. Consistent descriptive references to all the sessions include: *relevant, sets tone, helps focus, thought-provoking, stimulating, informative.* But there were two critiques of the readings: *too many and too time-consuming* (especially for *Session 1*) and *the readings were not referred to enough in the discussions.*

On the Comfort Level of the Group

In this instance, the evaluations were all very positive. I offer the following sampling of phrases used to describe the quality of group life: *openness, non-threatening, accepting, quieter ones are starting to speak up, supportive, growing together as a group, disagreements handled in non-judgemental ways, again tonight – a revitalizing, renewing experience on our shared journey.* Michael commented at the end of *Session 2* on the make-up of the group, accounting perhaps for some of the effective chemistry operating in the group dynamics:

> There is a good mixture of people in this room who have a good background: guidance, business, religion, social

sciences . . . and a good variety of different types of people dealing with different types of kids—some advanced, some general. This is a good mixture for this type of discussion.

On the Prayer Component

The evaluative comments for the prayer for each session were positive as well. Prayer was appreciated by everyone, but it is clear in the evaluations that some placed a higher premium on prayer than did others. Some comments: *the prayer sheds light on the theme for us as Catholic educators, gives us the gospel connection, celebrates our gifts, takes the conversation beyond just the discussion level, a very reflective way to begin our sharing, a time to focus, time to unwind and relax.*

On the Learning Outcomes

To appreciate the impact of the shared-reflections on different members of the group, I present the following responses to the question, "What learning took place for you this evening?":

- The effectiveness of collaborative learning was brought home.

- I enjoyed exploring androcentrism and sharing the adult approach to being a member of the church.

- A beginning teacher observed: "I really admire how Joseph thinks and analyzes. He is able to hear something for the first time, think about it for a short time, relate it to a past experience and interpret it."

- Women must be included in all of the structures of the church.

- We need, as Catholic educators, to role-model evangelization.

- The best context for learning is the sharing of personal experiences.

- Sharing of experiences is good. We learn so much from each other and ourselves as we tell our stories.

- Reflection is so critical: without it experiences are lost; with it growth has a chance.

- Not very interesting tonight. I didn't learn anything.

- The use of metaphor and image to express our faith and feelings was fascinating.

My favourite descriptive is: "From our conversation I learned shared groping is the right way to go about it." This, for me, is an appropriate twist for Catholic educators on Thomas Groome's shared praxis. *Shared groping* underscores the important struggle dimension to Catholic education: there really are more questions than answers; hence the importance of interpretation. Nonetheless, in the sharing there is understanding and support, and there are life-giving moments of hope.

On Questions and Needs

- Our real problem: how do we apply all of this to our life and real day-to-day situations?

- We need to work more at significantly helping/training teachers to do what we are talking about with the kids. Mario's question is important: "Where do we go? As teachers, how do we present this to the students?" We tried to talk about that question but really didn't get to it.

- As Catholic educators—as women and men—we need to explore the injustices structured into the institutional church and structured into our Catholic school system in all its aspects..

- We need the church in different ways. The church takes on different meanings and values at different times in our life.

I remarked in Chapter 5 that my journal for each session was invaluable, in that it became the place and means for me to evaluate the process as an ongoing formation experience. But the teachers' oral and written evaluations of each session were equally important because they allowed me to make appropriate changes in the process where they were called for: to be more careful with the print quality of the hand-outs; to work at clarity and precision in reflection questions; to moderate the quantity of readings; to alter time or schedule for our meetings. But even more significantly, the oral and written evaluations became a measure for me—a qualitative gauge of the kinds of learning taking place and the pace of that learning (formation) in the group. For the teachers, the evaluation moments were especially moments for internalization; for example, the consideration of the question "What learning took place for me this evening?" was itself a moment of integration and internalization.

Evaluation of the Model

The final evaluation *(Session 8)* was basically a detailed, written assessment of the total experience—different elements of the experience—a review, essentially, of the elements already considered in the oral and written evaluations. It was an evaluation of the *process*, emphasizing the themes and learning moments. It was an evaluation of the *model*, looking at the experienced teacher-inexperienced teacher mix, number of sessions, facilitation. I will now briefly review this evaluation data pertaining to the effectiveness of the experience as a model for formation in the Catholic high school.

On the Themes for the Sessions

When asked to rank the most pertinent theme in terms of relevance, the beginning teachers identified *formation,* while the experienced teachers selected *interpretation*. The theme *Catholic culture* was also deemed to be very relevant for both groups.

"Should the selection of themes have been left to the group?" Both beginning and experienced teachers were quite content with the process as it was: that I had proposed the themes. Had the discussion-reflection sessions continued, the experienced teachers would have been comfortable in suggesting further themes.

The experienced teachers saw the experience very much as a process—another moment in their own formation, a deepening of their own sense of what it is to be a Catholic educator. Their reflections in the evaluation expressed a maturity of internalization. One beginning teacher identified the experience as a process; the others saw something new happening but are still working at internalizing the experience.

When asked to identify "a learning moment," an occasion in their teaching and day-to-day activities when they were able to draw on an insight or strategy that had come up in the sessions, the beginning teachers very readily offered specific instances. On the other hand, the experienced teachers were more likely to stretch that moment into a gradual change of perception or attitude or approach—changes they attributed to the sharing in the sessions.

On Practical Recommendations Regarding the Experience as Model of Formation

All agreed that *for all participants, the experience should be invitational*, although they believed that there is room for some challenging encouragement.

Regarding *the qualities important for "an experienced teacher"* in such a group: the beginning teachers emphasized *experience* while the experienced teachers suggested *humility*.

On the *"mix"—the beginning and inexperienced teachers together:* there is unanimous support for the mix. The ongoing formation nature of the experience was emphasized along with the spin-off effects of friendship, interaction and shared experience outside the group. The mutual enrichment— beginning and experienced teachers together—was mentioned by several teachers. The beginning teachers definitely appreciated the *experience* (understood in the sense of understanding of and wise reflection on one's own role as a Catholic educator) of their senior colleagues.

The *positive qualities of this model* of formation were identified as: community-building beyond the sessions, mutuality (all are teachers; all are learners), the size of the group—large enough for people not to feel too pressured to speak all the time, and the relaxed, non-threatening atmosphere.

Suggested *obstacles* that might hamper such a model of formation included: insufficient time to prepare and share; being forced or mandated to participate; lack of skilled facilitation.

There were suggestions regarding *facilitation*. The overall consensus was that there be one, non-participating facilitator for the duration of the experience. This would especially make for consistency; participants would know their own set roles and expectations. When asked about desirable traits in the facilitator and desirable approaches to facilitation, participants made the following suggestions:

- believe in this process, in this model;
- be totally committed;
- be patient: it is a process about evangelizing teachers;
- remain detached; don't enter in;
- create a friendly, comfortable, non-threatening atmosphere;
- make the theme and questions clear;
- don't allow the conversation to turn into a debate;
- facilitate, don't dominate; let the process do its job;

- do not be too directive; don't have already established results in mind;

- remember that the process is the key, not the product!

The teacher-participants were asked: "Could this model of formation take the place of, or complement and support, the OECTA Religion Course?" The consensus was that this model would *complement* the OECTA Course. It was also felt that for the candidates for teaching at the high school level, it would make a valuable component of the OECTA Religion Course, given the practical and experiential nature of the process.

I bring this section on the evaluation of the model to a close by having the teachers speak for themselves about their experience:

> Ann: I think it is a useful way to clarify views by shared experience and to become aware of viewpoints different from your own . . . and may be valuable to gain a new perspective. I think that we probably take some of those viewpoints and remember them and apply them in situations in the future.

> Michael: Especially for the new teachers, we need more facilitation, either from yourself or whoever is facilitating the session. This could be a component, almost a teaching part of the experience: go through articles with us and share your own experience. For new teachers with little or no experience, how are they going to bring experience if they don't have any? For older teachers it is different. I think more facilitation or input would probably be very beneficial to the new teachers.

> Donna: I think experience teaches you so much! It's good for those of us who have been around for a while: you get that freshness! After a while you become too comfortable. This gives you a jolt. I better wake up. And I think for those

teachers who are new: they need to hear that it is okay to put curriculum aside sometimes and deal with other issues, and to show the compassion they feel in class; that discipline isn't the first thing to be concerned with—or attendance. New teachers are questioning themselves so much as people and teachers: choice of occupation, curriculum, faith. This process is a vehicle for teachers to dialogue and question.

Mario: I like the fact that some of us as new teachers may not have the experience, and so it is good to hear other experiences, teaching experiences. It is good to hear how people who have been in it longer have dealt with situations. That is helpful. I also like this process: it is informal. I think it works well. As with the makeup of the group . . . young and old . . . so there are good new ideas and good old ideas. This is a good mixture.

Raymond: I think this is a good idea. I think it strengthens the community as school for both groups. Both groups challenge each other. I think the experience does help form new teachers and strengthens and clarifies the more experienced teachers. I would like to see something like this done ongoingly!

Joseph: I think this is good. Now I don't know if experienced teachers have any answers, but I think sharing confusion is a good thing. In a way, knowing that you have the same questions and confusion as others gives you a sense of confidence; that there isn't necessarily one right answer. I like the group. I really find it fun, and I think something like this should be fun. And the process is good. We have to think; we have to reflect on experience. It is also a questioning and accepting environment.

Marie: It is an excellent way to share experiences, to talk about problems, and to work out possible solutions. You don't always have the opportunity to sit down with this large a group of people and discuss in such a focused way without distractions. It is a very non-threatening environment. You are not afraid to express your views. And as a new teacher I really do learn from the more experienced ones.

Findings of a "Reflective Practitioner"

In my introduction to this book I refer to myself as a reflective practitioner. I like that identification a lot. I think that pretty much describes the way I approach my ministry as a priest-educator. As I was going about facilitating the sharing of reflections of some concerned Catholic educators on the vocation of the Catholic educator, I could not help but reflect on my own experience during these months—months of hard work, apprehension and wonderment. The findings I record here derive from a reflection on my personal experience in this formation project. I am confident, however, that these findings are grounded also, in a fairly objective way, in the experience itself.

On Formation

There are seven aspects of formation emerging from this experience that I feel should be underlined.

1. *Session 2* became for me a moment of truth. Initially, I intended to elaborate a model of formation for Catholic high school educators, emphasizing especially initial formation for beginning teachers. While I acknowledged that such an experience would also form, in an ongoing way, experienced teachers, my intention was to focus on the beginning Catholic educator. *Session 2* was, both upsetting and revelatory for me, in this sense: the experienced teachers seemed to be profiting more from the experience than the beginning teachers. My dilemma was to try to reconcile this impres-

sion with my original notion. Over some time I worked through the fact that what was happening, though not as I intended, was still very worthwhile and valuable. In my own mind then, I began to look at this experience as formation, both initial and ongoing, and the evaluations have given me confidence that a qualitative formation experience took place for both the beginning and experienced teachers.

2. I believe that the criteria set out for selecting the experienced teachers were especially helpful. The beginning teachers confirmed this for me in identifying *experience* as the quality most admired in the other teachers. The context and content of the sharing in the sessions definitely indicate that *experience* is an appropriate criterion: it is the experience of reflective persons open to sharing their own unique stories as Catholic educators. For me, important forming moments of this experience were the gestures of affirmation and encouragement extended by the experienced teachers. Such hospitality made the beginning teachers feel at home and equal in their roles as Catholic educators.

3. This process was a very practical experience in formation. Teachers were consistently keen and quick to make concrete applications to their own school situations.

4. The experience reinforces my fundamental intuition that a credible and relevant formation program for Catholic educators must give priority of place to:

   • the vocation of the Catholic educator;

   • the personal experience of the Catholic educator;

   • the life context of the Catholic educator in the Catholic school.

5. There is an essential mutuality to formation: teachers teach and learn from each other. In this sense, formation is an

authentic adult learning experience. For a formation in faith, the evangelizer is evangelized in evangelizing.

6. Given what I have said to this point about formation, it must be said that such an experience must be invitational. Principals cannot force, school boards cannot mandate, facilitators cannot cajole. Concerned Catholic educators must invite a person to be part of a reflective sharing experience.

7. There is a new urgency to Catholic education; there is a new ecclesial reality. In Chapter 1, I outlined the challenges to Catholic education issued by Kenneth Westhues and Martin Royackers to make of the separate school system, an alternative education system founded solidly on gospel values. I am absolutely convinced that the formation of Catholic educators must be the necessary first step in creating that alternative system.

On Experience

I refer above to the wonderment that was an integral part of my own experience during this formation project. A large part of this wonderment, I feel, is my gradual discovery of the depth and the riches of my own reflected experience and the depth and riches discovered in a colleague's reflected experience. One must underline the importance of *reflected experience*, as one teacher did in the evaluations: "Reflected experience is so critical: without reflection, experiences are lost; with reflection, growth has a chance." And I would add: with shared reflection, formation happens.

In Chapter 6, I discussed the question of the lack of experience on the part of the beginning teachers. This can be problematic, but it need not be so. I believe that this lack can be overcome with time and the confidence that comes with the acceptance and hospitality accorded by the experienced teachers. Certainly, familiarity with the dynamic of sharing one's own story helps to overcome hesitancy about one's lack of experience.

On the Process

In different aspects of the experience, several points of a more technical or methodological nature surfaced and are deserving of comment.

1. The importance of *structure* cannot be exaggerated. In the hurly-burly life of a high school, time is crucial. Teachers do not like to waste time. They appreciated the two hour time-limit to each session. Detailed planning and organization are needed; a hospitable, non-threatening environment, relevant themes, clear phrasing of the questions, and thought-provoking questions all contribute to the richness of the experience.

2. The *prayer* component is essential. For the teachers, prayer was a time to unwind and focus. A privileging of the Word of God gives the chance for the Word to speak to the teacher-participants in different ways; very definitely it connects them to the vocational dimensions of being a Catholic educator. My hunch is that a ten-minute prayer reflection in the intimacy of a shared-reflection group will be a strange but rich new experience for many teachers. (This type of prayer does not happen that often in most teachers' experience.)

3. *Reflection questions* of a more sensitive, autobiographical nature are best kept to the end of the group experience. A facilitator should also exercise judgement as to the openness and receptivity of the group for such questions.

4. Over the course of the experience I discovered the *significance of story* as an invaluable instrument for sharing the meaning of one's vocation as a Catholic educator. Likewise,

the use of symbol, image and metaphor was a freeing moment for me and for most of the participants and produced some wonderfully rich reflections on the church and what it means to be a teacher in the Catholic high school today.

5. Two questions surfaced in the evaluations: one touches on *facilitation* and recommends more input on the part of the facilitator; the other requests a more "how-to" approach in evangelizing students. I respect these questions, but I am unable to resolve them. They were both asked by beginning teachers and could be interpreted as a desire for more personal security, in the sense that input and "how-to" solutions will provide confidence. My feeling is that these questions should be left unresolved for now. Perhaps future experiences of this nature will shed more light on their resolution.

Questions and Surprises

Under the rubric of *findings,* there are questions and surprises for me emerging from the experience that should be identified.

1. *Time,* as I have remarked, is a crucial question for the participants. Taking into account sessions, preparation and evaluations, each teacher spent between 25 and 30 hours participating in the experience. While I feel convinced that it was time well spent and that such experiences are imperative if Catholic education is to become an alternative education system based on gospel values, it is still a considerable amount of time to ask of teachers given the present reality of school life. So the question should be asked: how can such an experience be integrated into the Catholic educator's school life without being the cause of more pressure and frustration? This is a formation question, but it is a

question that school boards and OECTA should be grappling with!

2.   Where there is the openness and the willingness to begin such an experience in the Catholic school, Mario's declaration comes into play: "This is hard to do on your own. Someone has to stimulate that reflection or force [in the sense of invite] you into it." The animation question is a question for staffs in different schools. Who will take the initiative to invite teachers to come together and reflect on their vocation as Catholic educators?

3.   How do we *reclaim sacramentality,* as both context and content for evangelizing in the Catholic high school? This, I believe , is a question that needs further practical theological attention.

4.   I was surprised at the teachers' "Catholic faith and Catholic approach" to life and to their profession. Sexual abuse scandals and other weaknesses of that order of the institutional church have not sent these teachers walking. As a cleric, I am too sensitive to *la bella figura* of the church—its image and reputation. The faith of the teacher-participants is, as Andrew Greeley found of Catholics generally, solidly grounded in the sacraments and in the profoundly rich Catholic heritage that the teachers want to pass on to their own children and their students.

5.   I was equally surprised at the firmness of the teachers in shucking off the *child* attitude and behaviour as members of the church. This was manifest in their critique of clericalism and their growing awareness of the androcentrism structured into church life.

6.   The women's issue is central to any discussion on or description of Catholic culture in North America today. The reflections and sharing on this question, too, are part of the

wonderment of the experience for me. But this surprise translates as well into a dilemma for Catholic educators. In our education, especially in the social justice components, we promote justice, dignity and equality. But some of the structures of our church deny this justice, dignity and equality. The tension, frustration and pain inherent in this dilemma must continue to be part of the cross of Catholic educators in the struggle to transform these structures.

7. In the discussion on formation, both beginning and experienced teachers found that "we learn a lot regarding techniques, classroom management strategies and tricks of the trade from other teachers." They were talking about *practical experience*. The teachers then used this *practical outcome* to validate the type of evangelizing formation taking place in our sessions—learning from each other in the stories and experiences shared on what it is to teach in a Catholic high school. Indeed, this is a practical formation.

8. *Humility* is the quality most respected by experienced teachers in the "experienced, committed teacher profile." This was surprising for me; yet, it should not be surprising since *humility* must be the primary quality in any agent of evangelization. Paul VI insists that the church evangelizes but begins by being evangelized itself. Leonardo Boff is able to critique the church because of the truth that the church is at the same time saint and sinner, in need of conversion and reform. The teachers' respect for *humility* indicates their openness and their own felt-need for ongoing conversion and ongoing formation as Catholic educators.

9. There is, finally, the surprise for me inherent in the *sophisticated level of interpretation*—both the awareness of the need to interpret and the degree of ability to interpret—of the experienced teachers in particular. My own theological journey has been influenced by David Tracy's idea of inter-

pretation as arriving at a relatively adequate understanding of truth amidst the plurality and ambiguity of our time and place. My instinct was that this interpretive spirit and attitude are indicative of the internalized adult faith of the follower of Jesus, and that such an interpretive approach should mark the evangelizer in the Catholic school. The manner in which these teachers perceived interpreting and the need to model interpretation as a significant element of evangelization was a further dimension to my wonderment.

Implications and Challenges

The evaluations indicate that this formation experience has been beneficial for the participants. Sharing "gropings," hopes and faith around Catholic education, over an extended period of time, has proven to be a positive, formative experience for both beginning and experienced teachers. And as a colleague and facilitator, it has been a profoundly rich experience for me as well. I have a more realistic understanding of some of the critical questions and issues now confronting Catholic education. I have a deeper practical appreciation of different aspects of the vocation of the Catholic educator. There are further implications of this formation experience that deserve to be highlighted.

Adapting This Model of Formation

In this research, I chose to concentrate on the Catholic high school for two reasons: it is my own proper context for ministry, so consequently I feel more at home in speaking about it and questioning it; and, given the proliferation of Catholic high schools in Ontario since 1985, I feel that the formation needs for many new teachers and for staffs generally are more acute at the high school level than at the elementary level. Having gone through this process, I am confident that this model could work in any Catholic high school, and indeed, in any Catholic school—*tout court*! The practicality of the model has been illustrated in this report. What is required, first and foremost, is a sensitivity to the *need* for formation—both initial and ongoing—for Catholic teachers. If the formation need is not perceived, the model really is redundant. Indeed, if the formation need is not perceived, then the particular Catholic school or school board is likely paying only lip-service to the mission of Catholic education, considering it merely in a cosmetic way.

Leadership and animation are also essential for this model to work effectively, although they need not be found in the same person. Leadership can come from an administrator, department head or any concerned Catholic teacher who perceives the need and sets out to find animation—in the form of either a person or a team. So leadership to initiate and animation to organize and facilitate are imperative.

One needs, as well, a healthy sense of what constitutes *the experienced, committed teacher:* a teacher who has the humility, openness and reflective wisdom to share with beginning teachers his or her own understanding and experience of what it means to be a Catholic educator. For schools with an insufficient number of beginning teachers, the experience can then become an experience in ongoing formation.

Concluding Challenges

In 1971, Catholics in the Province of Ontario made full funding of Catholic high schools a major issue in the provincial election. William Davis and the Progressive Conservatives were opposed to the extension of the Catholic school system. William Davis and the Conservatives won a majority of seats in that election, and many Catholic educators, in defeat, could only envisage the disappearance of Catholic high schools. Some Catholic high schools did cease to exist because of insufficient funding, but many others came into existence in the ensuing thirteen years due to the determination of Catholic school boards, the continued sacrifice of religious communities, the commitment to Catholic education of dioceses across the province, and the willingness of parents to pay tuition. There was the will to have Catholic education at the secondary level.

In June, 1984, William Davis announced the completion of the Catholic school system; funding would be extended to Catholic high schools. Many Catholic educators celebrated this victory, but some wondered if government funding might not be more curse than blessing. What would happen to the *sacrifice* dimension? What about the special spirit, deriving from the charism of religious communities, that characterized many schools? How were these intangibles to be assured in the newly centralized, publicly administered Catholic high schools? I believe that the most critical question emerging now is: "Who is to see to the formation of Catholic teachers?"

The Catholic education community *resisted* from 1971 to 1984 in order to keep the Catholic high school reality alive. That resistance was marked by political lobbying, economic sacrifice and some extraordinary commitment on the part of trustees, teachers, parents and clergy. But a *new resistance* is called for in the 1990s if the education offered in the Catholic high school is to truly reflect what I have described as the *Catholic character* of the school. This new resistance has to do with the mission of Catholic education for our time and place, and the vocation of the Catholic educator. I believe that formation is at the very heart of the new resistance.

Catholic school trustees and administrators must be the leaders of the new resistance. They have the *trust* of the mission of Catholic education in their hearts and minds and hands. A fundamental question for them should be: "What makes a Catholic teacher a Catholic teacher? Is it only: 'Be a Catholic; have a pastoral reference; and take the religion course at the Faculty of

Education?'" There has to be more! *Formation* and *openness to formation*—initial and ongoing—is essential. Part of the vital trust for Catholic school trustees and administrators must be tending to the vocation dimension of Catholic teachers. The 1984 extension victory for the Catholic community will prove to be very hollow if it is not reinforced, inspired and infused by a dominant preoccupation with the formation of Catholic educators.

The Ontario English Catholic Teachers' Association (OECTA) must be considered a major partner in the Catholic education community in Ontario. I believe that OECTA must take much more responsibility for tending to the vision and mission of Catholic education. The real problem of Catholic education today is far beyond the dollars and cents, contractual questions that seem to take up so much of the time and energy of the OECTA leadership. The real problem is at the level of vision and mission. In this regard, the problem needs theological attention, addressing both the mission of the association and its local units, and the ongoing faith formation of its members. How refreshing, renewing and hopeful it would be to see *ongoing faith formation* for Catholic teachers as a central issue in contract negotiations.

Within the Catholic high school, *the principal* is the most important pastoral agent. The formation of new teachers and the ongoing formation of the other teachers should be a primary concern. For every principal, the important beginning-of-every-year question should be: "How is this teaching community going to grow in awareness of what it means to be Catholic educators?" Certainly, the model of formation elaborated here, or one like it, is a solid and very helpful approach in responding to that question.

And there is finally, an enormous challenge to *church leadership*. About ten years ago, in an essay on the university,

Northrop Frye likened the dynamics of education to the dynamics of driving. The prudent driver has eyes on the road ahead, but must constantly be aware of what is behind: alert to the rear-view and side-view mirrors. So it is with education. Education prepares students for the future, but it can do so only by constant reference to the past—to history and the stuff out of which the present has come to be.

In thinking about Catholic education, I like to play with a variation on the analogy of the windshield/rear-view mirror. I think of mountain driving in Alpine countries. Approaching a hair-pin curve, there is often a strategically-placed mirror that allows the driver to see what is ahead; what is in the future. In the church and church life in the Catholic school today, we are in many respects at just such an Alpine curve. Catholic educators are looking into the future of the church each day in dealing with the needs, hopes, questions and situations of their students. There is much about the future they could share with church leadership, I believe, regarding the reclaiming of sacramentality and a greater access to sacramentality in the schools—if it is true that the schools for many are now the primary place where young people experience the church. Catholic educators, particularly women Catholic educators, have much to share with church leadership regarding justice and equality for women and the pain caused by structures and regulations that exclude. This experience is vitally urgent because much of it derives from their female students—the future of the church!

And there is much essential to their ongoing formation that Catholic educators look to receive today from church leadership. Many committed teachers want their faith nourished by relevant preaching and meaningful liturgy. And many thoughtful Catholic educators, aware of their own vocation and ministry in the church, look for respect, understanding and support as they journey through many of the unavoidable, interpretive dilemmas deriving from the plurality and ambiguity that so mark our time and place.

Appendix 1

Sessions

Appendix 1.1 List of Readings

Session 1: On Social Analysis

- Various news clippings on violence towards women / materialism / food banks / media and television programming / rock music / moral illiteracy / marketing and teens.

- From Reginald Bibby's *Mosaic Madness,* Chapter 7: "The Institutional Casualty List."

Session 2: On Individualism

- From Reginald Bibby's *Mosaic Madness,* Chapter 5: "Success in Excess."

- An article by Tom Harpur, September 15, 1991, *Toronto Star*: "It's time whining Canadians focused on our real blessings."

- A feature essay by Albert Nolan, OP, in *Catholic New Times*, December 2, 1990: "The change you need is from individualism to community."

Session 3: On Catholic Culture Today – Part One

- Jack Costello, SJ, "Towards an Adult Church," *Compass,* January, 1990.

- From Eugene Kennedy's *The Now and Future Church:* "The Shape of Things to Come," pp.173-185.

- Andrew Greeley's feature essay in the April 12, 1991 *National Catholic Reporter*: "Sacraments keep Catholics high on the Church."

- Richard McBrien's article: "If conservatives are few, whom do bishops lead?" in the October 11, 1991 *National Catholic Reporter*.

Session 4: On Catholic Culture Today -Part Two

- Continue with Eugene Kennedy's "The Shape of Things to Come."

- From the publication *Miriam's Song II:* Elizabeth Johnson's "Recovering Women's Faith Experience From Scripture."

- The "Theological Elements" document created from the reflections of *Session 3.*

Session 5: On Evangelization

- From James Mulligan's *Evangelization and the Catholic High School,* Chapter 2: "A Meditation on Evangelization" (on six key passages from Paul VI's *Evangelii Nuntiandi*).

Session 6: On Interpretation

- Document created from examples of "the need to interpret" which came up during the first five reflection sessions.

Session 7: On Formation

- From the Ontario Bishops' *This Moment of Promise:* "Exhortation to Teachers."

- From John Paul II's *Vocation and Mission of the Lay Faithful,* Nos. 58 – 60: on the vocation and formation of the laity.

- From the Gospel of John, Chapter 15: on the ongoing need to be pruned. In this chapter, Jesus compares himself to a vine, and we, his followers, are the branches. As disciples, as the followers of Jesus, we need to listen often to the Word. It is in this prayerful listening that the Lord "prunes" us, as branches on the vine are pruned, so that we may bear even more fruit.

- From *Lay Catholics in Schools: Witnesses to Faith,* No. 32: on the personal witness of teachers.

- From Paul VI's *On Evangelization in the Modern World,* No. 18: on the need for conversion.

Appendix 1.2 Sample Reflection Questions

Session 2

Questions For A Reflection On "Individualism and Catholic Education"

Readings:

- Reginald Bibby's *Mosaic Madness,* Chapter 5: "Success in Excess."

- Tom Harpur's "It's time whining Canadians.... "

- Albert Nolan's "From Individualism to Community," especially Part 2.

- My *Evangelization and the Catholic High School,* pp. 74-79: ideology of individualism and ideology of relativism.

Note: The Albert Nolan article is, I think, very applicable to our discussion of individualism and Catholic education.

Reflection Questions:

1. Formulate the way you understand "the cult of the individual."

2. How do you experience "the cult of the individual" in your own life?

3. How do you see it operative in the ways we do Catholic education? Do you think we are any different on this score than our counterparts in public education?

4. How can we begin *to shuck off* the cult of the individual for ourselves and for our students?

5. A key personal conviction about Catholic high school education: I believe that the beginning Catholic high school teacher needs formation that develops within her or him the understanding that education is *more effective* and *more in keeping with the gospel ethic* when it is done *cooperatively.* Do you agree? If so, how do we go about this?

6. Other questions that should be dealt with: (Participants suggest.)

Appendix 1.3 Sample Prayer Reflection

Session 3

"On Catholic Culture Today"

Seasons —time and weather and climate can at times be a useful metaphor to understand where we are: as individuals in life; as a group in the institutional life of a Catholic school, or the institutional life of the church.

Ecclesiastes 3:1-8 — On time

John 12:20-28 —A November-type prayer. Jesus foretells his death and subsequent resurrection.

* *A question to keep in the back of your mind as we reflect this evening: what season do you think best reflects where we are now as church?*

Appendix 2

Theological Elements Document

Session 3

On Catholic Culture Today

Some Theological Elements

1. How would you answer Andrew Greeley's question? One of the readings was an NCR feature length article by Andrew Greeley on "why Catholics remain Catholics" (April 12, 1991, p. 12).

We presented the respondents with a variety of reasons for being Catholic . . .

- an explanation for life;
- rules on how to love;
- religious certainty;
- the rich heritage of the past;
- a faith to pass on to children;
- consolation in times of sorrow;
- the support of a community;
- something to bind the family and marriage together;
- the sacraments;
- parish life and activities;
- strong religious authority;

- help from priests;

- infallible papal teachings.

In the reflection, the consensus was that *sacraments / Catholic heritage / a faith to pass on to their children* were the reasons for being and remaining Catholic. *Sacraments* and the liturgy—both the personal and community dimension of it—would come up often in the reflection as things that are rich and to be treasured.

Faith is a constancy; there is continuity with the past.

> Joseph: I like the rich heritage of the past. When I think of my Catholic heritage I tend to think of my parents and grandparents... they are the people who taught me... it came from them. I am tied to my parents... the way I live my life... the way they lived theirs. After they were dead... they in a sense became more important... the tie with the past... the constancy of belief... within that structure. I like the idea of continuity of belief. I have a faith that goes beyond the institutional church. I see that the sacraments are the prime thing we need the institutional church for.

Faith is like the seasons... growing and sustaining... meaning something in different ways at different times.

> Donna: My faith is a lot like the seasons in the prayer we did. My faith changes as my life changes. Just this past Sunday there was the inscription service for the Grade-Two's at church, and that takes on a new meaning for me... the first communion for my child. The sacrament is richer now. I didn't have a strong Catholic background. But with these moments... my hope is that my kids will have one. And this is a source of strength for me now... as my parents get older and as I go through different seasons. I believe that my faith will be a great help to me.

2. The faith of the 1950s.... There was a lot that was cultural about it: vote Liberal; Irish versus Orangemen; don't date non-Catholics. So much of it was "cut and dried." The Jack Costello article in *Compass,* January 1990, "Towards an Adult Church," occasioned this reflection on the church of the 1950s. The *pedestal of clericalism* was expanded on anecdotally: "Father might have had the personality of an old tea towel, but he got automatic respect and was always taken care of first." It became very clear how cultural this pedestal of clericalism really was and is.

3. Marisa brings up the Newfoundland experience—the sexual assault charges brought against some priests and brothers—that became the point of departure for the reflection, "Towards an Adult Church." Marisa was there during the televised hearings. Here is where a lot of the *parent/child* discussion comes into

play. Through stories and anecdotes they relate how they want to shuck off the child in them that accepts the dictates of parent clergy.

> Ann: This spring we visited our son in X-ville. His wife isn't Catholic, and I don't think B. has been going to Mass that regularly. But because we were coming he found out what time Mass was and indicated he was going to go with us. So we went to church... and this priest... he put down women... he put down homosexuals... he attacked a couple of political parties... and I think he also worked on new immigrants. And when we came out of church, I was thinking and hoping that maybe he would go back again. But why would you ever go back there? I wouldn't go back to that church! And I was thinking... did I have a responsibility to go up to this man... and he wasn't old... maybe 40... and tell him that I really disagreed with what he said? I didn't. But I was mad at myself after... that I really didn't have the guts to do it.

In the discussion after Newfoundland, the central question seemed to be: How much of this faith was based on respect for clergy... roles... authority... structure... and how much of it was deeper... personalized... not dependent too much on the institutional structure?

4. In the sharing there were stories of a *personal synthesis* arrived at in faith. This should be understood in this way: some relativize the clergy and the institutional church. Faith is very personal; it is mystery; this happens most in the sacrament. The priest "is tuned out."

> Michael: We have had some poor priests, too, where I go to church and we still have some. But I never thought of it. I'm devout. I go every week. Some priests I don't like at all. I don't like their sermons. I tune out. And sometimes I leave Mass and I don't feel much. I didn't listen to him. But I say to myself: I didn't go to church to listen to the priest. I listen to the Mass! If I don't like the priest, I don't listen to him. I say to myself... the church... going to Mass is more to me than the human aspect of it. I read about the human aspects... that bothers me... but the church is more than human priests.

Michael fits very well into Greeley's thesis that it is the "sacraments that keep Catholics high on the church." In the evaluation, Raymond expressed how much he appreciated the Greeley article: "I found it to be an excellent summary of what it means to be a Catholic."

There seemed to be a consensus that *we can't stand by anymore and let such priests get away with abuses of power. We have to take ownership and accept our responsibility in the church.* At the same time it was said that *the institutional structure has got to clean up its act and tell such priests that they are out of line and they need to be rejuvenated.*

5.   Around the discussion on *sacrament* great emphasis is placed on the sense of community and the importance of participation. Communal prayer and liturgy should be relevant—speaking to the needs of people and where people are at (especially the kids in school); there is appreciation too, for the sacred... quiet... joy in the celebration.

> Marie: At college... we had 10:00 p.m. Mass on Sundays. Dimmed all the lights. There was a real sense of community; it was traditional, but the students were all involved. It was an important thing to do on Sunday night. It was the sense of community.

The appreciation for *community and participation* is the connecting point between those who experienced the pre-Vatican II church and those who know the church only in the last three decades. For the former, when the , liturgy is done well it is *freeing and enriching;* for the latter, it is *meaningful.* For both, when there is an absence of *community and participation* it is stifling, mediocre, boring, irrelevant.

6.   Question 2 for reflection: Think of a symbol... an image... a metaphor... of what it is to be a Roman Catholic today.

> Arthur: Does this make any sense?—something like you're out on the ocean. I like being on water... so you are out there floating around... but eventually you want to get back to land. I think there are a lot of Catholics these days who are asking a lot of questions... searching themselves... looking around. They are not really sure about their faith... but it's there, and you can always go back to it. I don't know... you're adrift on the ocean... but you can always go back to it.

Arthur describes the free-floating situation today of many Catholics... but at the same time he sees *church and faith* (not always distinct) as land: "solid" and "constant"—a place to come home to. The meaning here seems to be that church is more faith and sacramental experience; church makes meaning for people. It is not church in the hierarchical or institutional structure.

> Joseph: The image I have... I saw it in terms of building a house, you know. I saw... kind of the church as foundation ... and in the past... like for my parents it was the whole house... and there were rooms that were set... things that you were supposed to believe in. Everything was set. And you just moved into the house and lived there... and you lived in the rooms as they were set. Where... my church... I still think I have the same foundation... but all the materials are lying around, and I have some real

serious input into the way that church is going to be. And if I want to set it up that way... if I want to use what the church has to offer me... if I want to use the sacraments in a way that will be helpful to me... if I want to use clergy for interpretation and help... then I'll use them that way. But Catholics should be able to structure their own... on that foundation... they should be able to structure their own rooms and structure their own passageways so that it kind of is their own faith within a general structure. I grew up believing that there are certain dogmas... certain truths that are stable. But there is a whole interpretation of how we apply this to our lives and so forth. I really see a creative element that is part of our faith.

Joseph's image is a house. We have the pre-Vatican II and post-Vatican II churches in relief. Foundation is important, but then so is an adult synthesis. Here too, the *adult/parent* paradigm is operative and useful for understanding both church and faith. Throughout Joseph's image is the personal ownership and interpretation that are necessary. A creative dimension is very much at work in believing today and in membership in the church.

Joseph's image occasioned some questioning from Raymond. Isn't this really Reginald Bibby's cafeteria-type church membership that he describes in *Fragmented Gods* or *Mosaic Madness*? The consumer approach to religion... pick and choose what attracts you, etc.?

At this point, I intervened. I felt that Joseph's question and image are more than that. They are hermeneutical and touch the central fact that faith must be owned and personalized. "The child must grow up and leave the parent." This is creative. And living that faith means relativizing, that is, treating as non-important or even seeing as obstacle many of yesteryear's things of the faith, and things still proposed today at times by the institutional church (e.g., clergy on a pedestal). Joseph was in agreement with my interpretation.

> Raymond: It's hard trying to think of an image. I guess for me it's more the community... the struggling community. Not in the sense of just accepting something because someone told you, but rather... yes! This is really important. What does it mean to my life... to our life? There is a truth there that we will know by talking... by sharing. I really believe strongly that the Spirit is there working and moving among all of us. It's not that I accept it because someone else tells me... but we work it out together.

Raymond's emphasis is on community. The church is the Spirit present and active among us as believers questioning and sharing. Truth is present, but can only be arrived at and understood within the honest struggle of the community.

7. On the essentials of being a Roman Catholic today. Here I set the context and I quote from my journal:

I think a big problem facing Catholic education today and even more in the future is the question of the *unchurched or nominal Catholics.* We have Catholic schools; our kids are all baptized... but so many of them have received very little at home; they might hit a church maybe once a year. Our task as Catholic educators—to share with them as much as we can our heritage as Roman Catholics.

Thirty years ago, Catholics in Ontario had access to a system of shared symbols and values and meaning: sacramentals, devotions, family prayer, moral absolutes, holy days, consecrated bread and wine, a sense of sin, generally a sense of one's vocation in life as a Catholic. These symbols and shared meaning were knit together by regular Sunday practice on the part of families. Today's Catholic youth and young adults are too frequently growing up in an areligious environment with little or no contact with church life in the parish. They are not being socialized into "the Catholic way," "the Catholic reflex." They consequently have no access to, nor have they come to possess, the renewed (since Vatican II) shared symbols, values and meaning of the Catholic community.

So – the questions are: What is essential in being Roman Catholic today? And of these essentials—what perhaps can we pass on to the unchurched kids in our schools?

Raymond again emphasizes the central importance of community. "If kids do not have access to a system of shared meaning, etc., it is because we as the adult community are not doing it."

Joseph remarks on the fundamental/foundational importance of the initiation sacraments: baptism and Eucharist. "Even the unchurched *know* they have been baptized and can go to communion." There will come a searching-for-meaning time later in adult life. Then they will go back to retrieve some of the meaning experienced at key moments in their early and adolescent apostolic/liturgical sacramental life.

- It is generally agreed that *access* to a system of shared meaning is not frequently found in families today.
- But even thirty years ago—that system of shared meaning had roots that were suspect! There was a lot of cultural stuff attached to it, as we have already seen.

And there is the question too: *What is the "Catholic reflex"?*

There are some interesting reflections describing "the Catholic reflex":

- It is changing; it still does kick-in; it is being nurtured especially in *experiences,* both liturgical and sacramental.

- Involvement and participation are critically important.

- It manifests itself more often now in a faith that acts, more than in the past when faith for some was passive.

- There is a strong *social justice face* to the Catholic reflex.

- It sometimes does not surface until years later during the search for meaning.

- Signs and physical, cultural symbols are still important: icons, enthroned scripture, candles.

- It is passed on by *the force of personal witness and actions* rather than by lectures and words.

- When kids are vulnerable... this is the really *teachable moment* to pass on the Catholic reflex.

8. Our prayer this evening focused on *seasons.* We prayed Ecclesiastes 3:1-8 on time... and John 12:20-28 in which Jesus foretells his death and resurrection. As a prelude to the prayer, I commented that time and weather and climate can at times be a useful metaphor to understand where we are as individuals in life and as a group, where we are in the institutional life of the church. I asked them to keep this question in the back of their minds: *What season do you think best reflects where we are at now as church?*

- Joseph thought "winter." Many ways and ideas are dying; decreasing number of priests; new models are being born—parish and bishop negotiating regarding a new pastor. People drive now for comfort and meaning in liturgy.

- Arthur agreed. "Winter!" There are things that have to change or will change.

- Marisa remarks on the gray areas in between the seasons.

- Ann works out of Ecclesiastes: a time for keeping... a time for throwing away... a time for knocking down... a time for building up. Ann's critical questions: What are we going to keep? What are we going to throw away and what are we going to leave behind because we have outgrown it?

- Raymond likes Marisa's in-between seasons. Winter into spring. There is hope in the new life, the fresh sprouts, the greening, but winter remains with the blanket of snow and galoshes that can trample the sprouts! But it is inevitable—the new growth will eventually push aside the dead leaves.

- Michael likes the consistency of summer... warm breezes. This is what he finds in his parish. It is consistently satisfying as summer is consistently nice.

- Gregory comments that the heat waves of summer can be the church under fire, and the harvest moon signals that change must come.

- For Marie it is spring. Spring means new life. We are forced to make changes. We are not touching younger people.

- For Donna, Ecclesiastes is significant: a time for healing, a time for searching, like spring—a time for renewal and a fresh start.

Index